Puss in Boots

A Pantomime

Alan Brown

Samuel French - London
New York - Toronto - Hollywood

CHARACTERS

Puss in Boots
Jill
Jack, the Knave of Hearts
Mr Tap, the teacher
Colin
Gilbert ⎱ his brothers
Filbert ⎰
Ferdinand, the King of Hearts
Gertrude, the Queen of Hearts
Cobbler
Oswald, the Ass
Woodcutter
Princess Rosalind
Princess Isabel
Blunderbore, the Ogre
Lion
Katranah, the Queen of the Gypsies
Villagers, Children, Animals of the Forest, Ghosts, Guards,
   Gypsies, Attendants, Peasants

PROLOGUE

ACT I

ACT II

AUTHOR'S NOTE

The use of the scenic-book device eliminates the need for Black-outs at the end of each scene, and of course any delays while scenery is flown, thus adding considerable impetus to the performance.

However, it is by no means indispensable, and if preferred, the pantomime can be performed with the traditional alternate full-stage and front-cloth scenes as follows:

No Prologue

ACT I

ACT II

MUSICAL NUMBERS

PROLOGUE
Music   Orchestra

ACT I

Song 1	Villagers, Children, Jill
Music: "Jingle Bells"	Orchestra
Song 2 "Hail To His Majesty"	Children, Gilbert, Filbert, Mr Tap
Music: "Boys And Girls Come Out To Play"	Orchestra
Song 3	Gerty, Children, Jack, Ferdy, Gilbert, Filbert
Song 4	Jack, Jill
Song 5	Colin
Music	Orchestra
Song 6	Rosalind
Song 7 "What's For Dinner?"	Ferdy, Gerty, Jack, Isabel, Rosalind
Song 8	Colin
Music: reprise of Song 8	Orchestra
Song 9	Rosalind
Music: reprise of Song 8	Orchestra

ACT II

Music	Orchestra
Song 10	Ghosts
Song 11 "We Must Be Ever So Quiet"	Gerty, Jack, Ferdy, Audience
Song 12 "Hokey Pokey"	Blunderbore, Gerty, Jack, Ferdy
Music: reprise of Song 8	Orchestra
Song 13	Rosalind
Song 14	Gerty and Ferdy, Jack, Jill, Colin, Isabel, Rosalind
Reprise of **Song 1**	Company
Finale	Company

Alan Brown has produced a list of song suggestions which is available free of charge upon application to Samuel French Ltd.

A licence issued by Samuel French Ltd to perform this pantomime does NOT include permission to use any copyright songs and music in the performance.

The notice printed below on behalf of the Performing Right Society should be carefully read.

The permission of the owner of the performing right in copyright music must be obtained before any public performance may be given, whether in conjunction with a play or sketch or otherwise, and this permission is just as necessary for amateur performances as for professional. The majority of copyright musical works (other than oratorios, musical plays and similar dramatico–musical works) are controlled in the British Commonwealth by the PERFORMING RIGHT SOCIETY LTD, 29–33 BERNERS STREET, LONDON W1P 4AA.

The Society's practice is to issue licences authorizing the use of its repertoire to the proprietors of premises at which music is publicly performed, or, alternatively, to the organizers of musical entertainments, but the Society does not require payment of fees by performers as such. Producers or promoters of plays, sketches, etc., at which music is to be performed, during or after the play or sketch, should ascertain whether the premises at which their performances are to be given are covered by a licence issued by the Society, and if they are not, should make application to the Society for particulars as to the fee payable.

COPYRIGHT INFORMATION

(See also page ii)

PROLOGUE

As the CURTAIN *rises the stage is bare, except for a giant book at the back of the stage which bears the title* PUSS IN BOOTS, THE STORY OF A CLEVER CAT

Music

Puss's head appears round one side of the book from behind. He waves to the audience. He disappears, then his head appears round the other side of the book. Again he waves to the audience. He comes out from behind the book, and does a cocky little dance which brings him downstage. He waves to one or two children in the audience. He points to the book and indicates that this is all about him. "Puss in Boots"—that's him! "The Story of a Clever Cat"

He dashes off and returns with a noticeboard and a fishing-rod. The noticeboard is attached to an artificial ice-crack and reads: DANGER! NO SKATING! *but the "NO" has been crossed out. He places this upstage. The fishing-rod's line is attached to an artificial hole. He places this downstage to one side and sits there fishing. Then he notices the book is still closed. He opens the first page of the book to its full width. It represents the exterior of an old water mill. He returns to his fishing-rod and continues fishing*

ACT I

SCENE 1

The exterior of the old mill

Song 1

The song is a skating melody. Villagers and Children enter skating and singing, using the stage as if it were the frozen mill pond. Jill, the Gypsy, enters carrying a bucket, and joins in the singing

If the Prologue has been used, Puss exits during the number, taking the fishing-rod

Towards the end of the song, Jill exits with her bucket

1st Child Look! Look! It's Jack.
2nd Child The Knave of Hearts!

The Children all giggle with laughter

3rd Child Looking for Jill the Gypsy.

They giggle again

Jack, the Knave of Hearts, enters

Children (*chanting*) The Knave of Hearts, the Knave of Hearts,
             He stole the tarts, he stole the tarts,
             All on a summer's day.
             But Gypsy Jill, with Cupid's darts
             Did steal his heart away!
             Yes, Gypsy Jill, with Cupid's darts
             Did steal his heart away!
Jack I say, you kids! That's not very respectful you know!
Children No, Your Highness.
Jack After all, I am a prince.
Children Sorry, Your Highness.
Jack That's more like it.
1st Child You seem very cross this morning, Your Highness.
2nd Child You must have got out of the wrong side of bed.
Jack Well what else could I do? I didn't want to climb over Mater and Pater.

The Children giggle

    Actually, I'm looking for Jill, the Gypsy.
1st Child Well, *actually*, Your Highness, we saw her just a moment ago.

2nd Child She went up the hill.
3rd Child To fetch a pail of water.
Jack What right up there? Oh, all right!

Jack exits

1st Child Poor old Jack.
2nd Child She'll never marry him while Colin's around.

The Children play a lively game of leapfrog on the ice, to the music of "Jingle Bells", waving their arms madly after each jump as if to keep their balance. Perhaps one falls. Suddenly there is the loud crashing sound off, of a bucket

Jack comes falling on to the stage with the bucket, followed by Jill. They finish in a heap

Jack (*rubbing his head*) Oooh! Oooh!
Children (*holding hands, and dancing round them, singing*)
Jack and Jill, went up the hill,
To fetch a pail of water.
Jack fell down, and broke his crown,
And Jill came tumbling after.

Jack tries to rise, but slips down again

Then up Jack got, and home did trot,
As fast as he could caper.
He went to bed to mend his head,
With vinegar and brown paper.

The Children laugh

Jack Oh I say, buzz off, you kids.
Jill Are you satisfied?
Jack I'm sorry, Jill. I only wanted to carry the water for you.
Jill Well, where is it?

Jack goes to the bucket

Jack (*taking out a solid block of ice*) Here you are, Jill.
Jill What's this supposed to be? It's frozen.
Jack It'd make a lovely ice-lolly!
Jill Ohh! (*She throws it off*) You're hopeless. Why do you always follow me everywhere? You know the Queen has forbidden it.
Jack I love you, Jill.

The Children giggle

Oh go away!
Jill Don't be so silly!
Jack I do! I want to marry you. (*Sadly*) I know I haven't got much money. We're frightfully hard up at the palace.
Jill Doesn't the Queen give you any pocket money?
Jack Yes, of course.

Jill Well, you should have saved it.

Jack I did. Every week the Queen made me put a shilling into a little black box.

Jill Well?

Jack It wasn't till I was twenty-one I found out it was the gas meter.

The Children laugh

> *Jack and Jill exit, taking the bucket with them*

> *A bell is heard ringing, and Mr Tap, the teacher, enters ringing the school bell. Mr Tap is a kindly old gentleman with whiskers*

Mr Tap Come along, children. Come along. Time for school now.

Children (*soulfully*) Ooooh!

1st Child When are we going to get a real school?

Mr Tap You've got a real school.

2nd Child I don't call that a real school. It's just an old mill.

Mr Tap Now, now. It's not what's in there that matters — (*he points to the mill*) — it's what's in there! (*He points to the child's head*) Anyway, I've got a surprise for you all. The Queen of Hearts is coming to visit the school today.

Children Hooray!

1st Child Will she bring us any presents?

Mr Tap If you are all very good, and very clever, she has promised to give you . . . do you know what?

2nd Child A holiday?

Mr Tap No, no, no. She has promised to pay for a brand new school!

Children (*disappointedly*) Oh!

Mr Tap So come along, let's get inside before Her Majesty arrives.

1st Child We can't. The miller's sons haven't arrived with the keys.

Mr Tap Are they late again? I'll have to speak to those boys.

A motor horn is heard, off, and cries of "Hurry up, Colin! Faster! Mush! Mush!"

> *Colin enters pulling a toboggan on which are squeezed his two silly brothers: Gilbert who is very long and mincing and Filbert who is very short. They carry their schoolbooks*

Gilbert Oh you are slow! I'm nearly frozen. Look at me fingers. Like a bunch of tutti-fruities!

Gilbert rises from the toboggan, his end of which rises into the air, tipping Filbert on to the ice

Filbert Hey! Have you done?

Gilbert (*giving Colin a push*) Now look what you've done! (*Pushing again*) You've upset Filbert!

Filbert (*pushing from the other side*) You've upset Filbert!

Gilbert (*pushing*) You're a clumsy clot!

Filbert (*pushing*) You're a clumsy clot!

Gilbert (*pushing*) You're a clumsy clot!
Filbert (*pushing*) You're a clumsy clot!
Gilbert There's a hell of an echo round here!
Colin (*shrugging them both off*) Please! That's enough.
Gilbert ⎱ (*together*) Oh! (*They fall down on the ice*)
Filbert ⎰
Filbert He's done it again.
Gilbert Oh I could spit.
Filbert He's done it again.
Gilbert Pick us up this instant.

Colin helps them with difficulty to their feet. They cling to him

Mr Tap Now, now. That's enough of that. We must get ready for the
 Queen's visit.
Gilbert ⎱ (*together*) The Queen!
Filbert ⎰

*Gilbert and Filbert fall down again in astonishment. Mr Tap helps them to their
feet*

Gilbert Did you say the Queen?

Gilbert and Filbert hang on to Mr Tap. There is a fanfare of trumpets

Mr Tap Too late. They're here.
Colin I'll unlock the mill.

He exits behind the mill, taking the toboggan with him

*The Children line up with Gilbert and Filbert who are still clinging to Mr Tap
and they sing*

Song 2. Hail To His Majesty

Children ⎞
Gilbert ⎟   Hail to His Majesty,
Filbert ⎟   King Ferdinand of Hearts.
Mr Tap   ⎠   Hail to Queen Gertrude,
                  Who made the royal tarts.
                  Hail to the head
                  That wears the royal crown;
                  Hail to Ferd and Gerty
                  They never let us down!

*Little King Ferdinand, who is bespectacled and very shortsighted, enters
pushing Queen Gertrude who is on roller skates. They both wear crowns*

Gerty Whatcher, peasants!

*But she is out of control. Ferdy can't stop her and she crashes into Mr Tap and
Gerty, Mr Tap, Gilbert and Filbert all fall down in a heap*

 Help!
Ferdy (*in his shortsightedness, helping to pick up Filbert instead of Gerty*) So

sorry, Gertrude, my dear. It was a knocksident—er—a smashion—a collide-up. Let me help you, my dear!

Filbert I'm Filbert.

Gerty Ferdy!

Ferdy Oh, I'm so sorry, an horror—I mean an error.

The Children help Gerty to her feet

Gerty Thank you, loves. I apologize for the old man. It's the National Health specs, you know. He's got the frames—he's waiting for the lenses. All right, Ferdy, I'm here. (*She takes Ferdy by the arm*) Coming here through the village, I caught him shaking hands with the village pump. I ask you—the village pump! Know what he said as I dragged him away?

Mr Tap No, Your Majesty?

Gerty "He's a nice old fellow, but doesn't he splash when he talks!"

Ferdy Well, my dear, anyone can mook a mistick—er—cook a mistook—er . . .

Gerty Yes, dear. Take a deep breath. (*To Filbert*) Where's the nearest boozer?

Gilbert You're talking to him.

Gerty (*giving Gilbert a look*) I shall remember you! Now then, my lords, ladies, gentlemen, and children. (*A large benevolent smile*)

Filbert (*sneezing*) Aaahtchoo!

Villager Bless you!

Mr Tap Quiet, children. Her Majesty is going to make a speech.

Gilbert Fags out everywhere!

Gerty My lords, ladies, gentlemen, and children. (*A benevolent smile*)

Filbert Aaarchoo!

Villager Bless you!

Gerty Haven't you got a hanky?

Filbert No, ma'am.

Gerty Well try a tissue.

Filbert Oh, right. (*Sneezing*) Ah tishoo!

Gerty (*to Mr Tap*) Have you reported this accident? Never mind. Now! My lords, ladies, gentlemen and children. (*A benevolent smile*)

Filbert Ahh——(*He stops*)

Gerty Really! Why don't you buy an inhaler?

Filbert I went to the chemist—they didn't have one.

Gerty Well try Boots!

Filbert I did, but me nose got stuck in the lace holes!

Gerty (*to Mr Tap*) A scholarship student no doubt! My lords, ladies, gentlemen, cheeldrenn (*a crocodile smile*) . . .

There is a rumble of thunder

Er . . . it gives me great pleasure . . .

Louder thunder, and the stage grows darker

1st Child (*pointing upwards into the audience*) Look! The Ogre!

Gerty slips up with fright, pulling down Ferdy, Mr Tap, Gilbert and Filbert who are clinging to each other in terror

Children ⎫
Villagers ⎬ (*screaming together*) The Ogre! The Ogre!

The Children and Villagers rush off behind the mill in terror

More thunder!

During the following, Ferdy, Mr Tap, Gilbert and Filbert scramble off behind the mill

Blunderbore is heard via front-of-house speakers

Blunderbore (*off; in stentorian tones*)
          Hear me, mortals! The time is nigh,
          For Blunderbore's own Christmas pie.
          But the dish will be no good
          Without a sauce of human blood.
          Your negligence has made me wild!
          Where's my annual Christmas child?
          I've eaten no-one for a year.
          My stomach feels distinctly queer.
Gerty (*sliding about towards the mill*) You're a wicked ogre! You'll have no more children from here! Why don't you leave us alone?
Blunderbore (*off*) Your Majesty will live to rue
          These words. Take care! I'll eat you too!
Gerty *Eat me?* Are you *serious* or was that meant to be a joke?
Blunderbore (*off*) I'm serious.
Gerty Good.
Blunderbore (*off*) Why?
Gerty I don't like them kind of jokes!

She staggers off behind the mill

Blunderbore growls and his voice dissolves into thunder

Puss enters nimbly and turns a page of the book to:

SCENE 2

The interior of the old mill

Puss exits, taking the noticeboard

The Children enter to the music of "Boys and Girls Come Out to Play". They carry long benches, a blackboard, easel, cane, etc. One comic bench has legs at one end and in the middle only. The Children sit on the other benches

Gilbert and Filbert enter and sit on the comic bench—Filbert at the legless end. Mr Tap enters and goes to the blackboard

Mr Tap Rise, children, for Her Majesty the Queen!

Gilbert and the Children rise. Filbert's end of the bench collapses and he falls on the floor

Filbert!

Filbert goes to Mr Tap and holds out his hand. Mr Tap gives him a tap with the cane. Filbert returns to his place

   Gerty enters, this time without her skates

Gerty Good-morning, children.
Children Good-morning, Your Majesty.

Gilbert, Filbert and the children sit

Mr Tap Rise, children, for His Majesty the King!

Gilbert and the Children rise. Filbert's end of the bench collapses again and he falls on the floor

Filbert!

Filbert goes to Mr Tap and receives another tap with the cane. He returns to his place

   Ferdy enters

Gerty Ferdy! You sit there (*She indicates Gilbert's and Filbert's bench*) It'll do you good to learn something. (*With a benevolent smile*) Sit, children!

They sit. Ferdy crosses and sits on Gilbert's knee. He feels Gilbert's leg

Ferdy I think the spring's gone in this one, dear.
Gerty Ferdy!
Ferdy (*realizing his mistake*) Oh, I pardonize—er—beg your apology.

He and Gilbert rise and Filbert is on the floor again. Filbert crosses to Mr Tap for his caning. Gilbert and Ferdy sit again. Filbert returns to his seat

   Jack enters, disguised as a schoolboy with a patch over one eye

Gerty Aha! A latecomer!

Jack goes to the blackboard, in the middle of which is a nail. Jack draws a half-circle up to the nail so that it looks like a hook. He hangs his hat on it. He goes towards Gilbert, Filbert and Ferdy

Make room for him, boys!
Ferdy }
Gilbert } (*together*) Certainly!

They rise and Filbert is on the floor again. He goes to receive his caning and then rejoins Jack, Gilbert and Ferdy on the bench

Gerty (*standing by the blackboard which has the letters of the alphabet on it*) Now then. I think that 'orrible Ogre's 'opped it, so if there are no more interruptions we can begin. I want to find out how ignorant you all are. So listen. (*She sings*)

Song 3

This develops into a full production number gradually involving the Children, Jack, Ferdy, Gilbert and Filbert and is an ideal opportunity for much comic business particularly concerning Filbert and the collapsing bench

At the end of the number, Filbert finishes up on the floor again and goes to receive his caning from Mr Tap. He is halfway back to his place when he stops suddenly and realizes something. He stands there with his feet crossed, one finger in his mouth, his other arm raised, looking at the Queen beseechingly and in distress. She sees him and cocks her head enquiringly. He goes and whispers in her ear, pointing to the exit. She nods her head

Filbert runs out quickly

Now then, General Knowledge. (*She points to Jack*) You, boy! What's your name?
Jack Bill.
Gerty No, no, no. Not Bill. Your full name. Not just a bit of it. I want your full name.
Jack Bill Brahn!
Gerty No, dear! You don't understand. You mustn't say "Bill". Little girl, what's your name?
1st Child Jenny.
Gerty And what's that short for?
1st Child Jennifer.
Gerty And you, dear. What do your friends call you?
2nd Child Maggie.
Gerty Maggie! And what's that short for?
2nd Child Margaret!
Gerty And you, love. What do they call you?
3rd Child Chris.
Gerty And what's that short for?
3rd Child Christine.
Gerty (*returning to Jack*) So now, little boy. What's your full name?
Jack Billious!

Filbert enters, and crosses the stage pulling a scrubbing brush on the end of a lead. He looks back towards it and whistles

Gerty Hello, it's the Brain of Britain. I say! Boy! Duckie!
Filbert Huh?
Gerty Nice little dog you've got there. What's his name?
Filbert You must be mad—this is a scrubbing brush.
Gerty Oh. I'm so sorry.
Filbert (*to the brush*) Aha! We fooled 'em there, Rover. Good boy! Come on, boy! Good boy!

Filbert exits with the brush

Gerty (*to Mr Tap*) What did I tell you. There are no flies on him!

Mr Tap No, Your Majesty.

Gerty Mind you, you can see where they've been. (*To Gilbert*) You there! Boy!

Gilbert My *name* is Gilbert.

Gerty Ah! Fine memory this boy's got. If you bought a dozen nuts, and you lost four, then you bought another dozen, and you lost six. What would you have?

Gilbert An 'ole in me pocket.

Gerty An 'ole in yer . . . You're not very bright are you?

Gilbert I come from a broken home.

Gerty Oh?

Gilbert Me parents were fastidious.

Gerty Uhuh!

Gilbert Me mother was fast——

Gerty ⎫ (*together*) ⎧ —and your father was hideous.
Gilbert ⎭   ⎩ —and me father was hideous.

Gerty Lovely. And what are *you* going to be when you leave school?

Gilbert Happy!

Gerty Uhuh! Anyone know any poetry?

Mr Tap Come along, children, poetry.

Jack (*rising*) Dramatic recitation!

Gerty Dramatic recitation!

Jack He called: "Isabel!" But she kept on running. (*Sadly*) He called: "Isabel!" But she kept on running. (*In tears*) He called: "Isabel!" (*Broken-heartedly*) But she kept on running.

Gerty Why?

Jack Her name was Maud. (*He sits*)

Gerty I see. Any questions?

Ferdy (*rising*) Yes, dear.

Gerty Oh, you've woken up, have you? Well?

Ferdy Three cornflakes on a plate: which one is the murderer?

Gerty Three cornflakes? Er . . . I don't know!

Ferdy Nor do I, it's a cereal! (*He chuckles with delight*)

Gerty You've been having them pains in the head again, haven't you!

Filbert enters

Filbert Oi! Can I come back now?

Gerty What's that?

Filbert Can I come back?

Gerty "*Can* I come back?" "*Can* I come back?" *May* I come back! Where's your grammar?

Filbert (*pointing to the audience*) Down there with me grandpa! (*He sits on the bench*)

Gerty (*to Mr Tap*) He's a bit of a clot, isn't he?

Gilbert A what?

Gerty I said "a clot".

Gilbert Clot?

Gerty Come here!

Gilbert goes to her. She spells out the word, accompanying each letter with a slap on the face

C—L—O—T! Clot!

Gilbert returns to his seat, rubbing his face

Filbert (*rising*) What did she say?
Gilbert She says you're an ignoramous.
Filbert A what?

Jack and Ferdy rise to watch as Gilbert slaps Filbert's face as he spells out the letters

Gilbert I—G—N—O . . . (*He pauses, uncertain, then continues*) O—P—Q—R—S—T—U—V—W—X—Y—Z! Clot!

Filbert sits on the legless end of the bench, falls, and goes to Mr Tap for his caning. He goes back to his place and they all sit

Gerty Well, I'm not very impressed with this lot, Tap!
Mr Tap I'm sorry, Your Majesty.
Gerty Never mind. I'll give you a new school just the same. It looks as if you need it. As for the rest of today . . .
Mr Tap Yes, Your Majesty?
Gerty You'd better all have a holiday!
Children (*cheering*) Hooray.

They all stand and cheer. Filbert falls on the floor again. Mr Tap rings his bell

To the accompaniment of "*Boys and Girls Come Out to Play*" the Children, carrying the benches, blackboard, easel, etc., exit, followed by Mr Tap, Gerty, Ferdy, Gilbert and Filbert

Jack remains and takes off his disguise

Jill enters

Jack Where have you been?
Jill Oh! I was looking for Colin.
Jack It's always Colin, isn't it?
Jill I don't know what you mean.
Jack I don't look as daft as I am, you know.
Jill It's no good, Jack. The Queen doesn't like me. After all, I'm just a common gypsy girl. (*She starts to go*)
Jack Don't go, Jill.
Jill I must. I have work to do.
Jack Stay here, just for a minute.
Jill Why?
Jack Well think of the weather out there. It's terrible.

They sing

Song 4

At the end of the song, Gerty enters, followed by Gilbert, who is carrying a will, and Filbert

Gilbert There he is!
Filbert That's him!
Gerty So it was you all the time! Bill Brahn, eh? Thank you, boys! And with that girl again!

She takes Jack by the ear and starts to lead him out

I've told you to keep away from gypsies. You never know where they've been.
Jack But, Mother . . .

They exit

Gilbert (*to Jill*) Oi, you! 'Op it!
Jill Are you speaking to me, you long streak?
Filbert Yes, you!
Gilbert Are you suggesting I'm thin?
Jill You look like a refill for a ball-pen.

She exits

Gilbert Nasty bit of Romany that!
Filbert What's up?
Gilbert She's insulated me!
Filbert That's got you taped!
Gilbert Has the teacher gone yet?
Filbert Mr Tap?
Gilbert Yes. Shrub-Mug.
Filbert Don't think so.
Gilbert Good, I've got it here.
Filbert Is the ink dry?
Gilbert Ssssh! (*Looking at the will*) Lovely handwriting I got, ain't I? Ssssh!
Filbert Ssssh!
Gilbert Ssssh! Let's get him.
Gilbert \
Filbert | (*together*) Mr Tap! Sir! Teacher!

Mr Tap enters

Mr Tap (*as he comes in*) Yes, children. What is it?
Gilbert We wondered if you could read this for us, sir.
Mr Tap What is it? (*He takes the will*)
Filbert We found it.
Gilbert It's our dear old father's will. (*He bursts into tears*)
Filbert (*also howling*) It tells us what he left us.
Mr Tap But this concerns Colin, too.
Gilbert |
Filbert | (*together*) Hardly! (*They giggle with delight*)

Colin enters

Mr Tap Ah, Colin. I have your father's will here.

Colin Oh? I didn't know he left one.

Mr Tap The spelling is terrible.

Gilbert Well, he wasn't very bright. He was a gentleman farmer.

Mr Tap A gentleman farmer?

Gilbert All he could raise was his hat.

Mr Tap Well it's very simple. (*Reading*) "I divides my property in free parts. To my dear Gilbert, my good clever, oldest son, I leaves me mill."

Gilbert Well fancy!

Mr Tap "To my dear Filbert, my dear little second son, I leaves Oswald, me ass."

Filbert Well I never!

Mr Tap "But to Colin, my naughty, wicked, horrible, youngest son, I leaves only Puss, the Cat!"

Colin (*taking the will from Mr Tap*) I don't believe he wrote this at all!

Gilbert (*snatching the will from Colin*) Don't show your ignorance!

Filbert I think it's jolly good!

Gilbert Anyway, there's nothing you can do about it.

Mr Tap I'll leave you boys to argue it out between you.

He exits

Gilbert Well, a cat's not much use to you, is it?

Filbert And it's not much use to us neither.

Gilbert Filbert's ass will be very useful.

Filbert He can give us milk.

Gilbert And work the treadmill.

Filbert And carry things.

Gilbert So Filbert can stay. But you——

Filbert —must go!

Gilbert Today!

Gilbert ⎱
Filbert ⎰ (*together*) At once!

Gilbert This is our mill now! We're having no more schools in it neither.

Filbert Hooray!

Gilbert If you'll take my tip, you'll drown that cat, and sell his fur.

Filbert To make mittens.

Gilbert Or a muff!

They both laugh

That's the only way you'll make money out of an animal like that!

Filbert Miffens!

Gilbert Or muffins!

They both roar with laughter and exit

Colin What am I going to do?

Puss enters

There, Puss, did you hear that?

Puss nods

You and I are on our own now. Come here, Puss.

Puss backs away in fright

No, no. Don't worry. I would never hurt you.

Puss hesitates

Come on! We're pals, aren't we?

Puss runs across to Colin and licks his hand

I'm your pal, and you're my pal. Right?

Puss nods and shakes hands

But what am I going to do? I need some sort of help.

Puss points to himself

You? How can you help me?

Puss taps his head

Oh, you're a clever cat, are you? And what are you going to do to help?

Puss kneels down and rubs his head against Colin's leg

Now what do you want?

Puss indicates he wants boots on his legs

Boots? On a cat? That's silly, Puss. Cats don't wear boots!

Puss mews and nods his head vigorously

But look. (*He produces a single coin*) That's all I've got in the world.

Puss strikes his chest

Oh, yes, *and* you, of course. I'm sorry. Still, it's not very much, is it? But somehow, Puss, I don't care. Do you?

Puss shakes his head. Colin sings

Song 5

At the end of the song the voice is heard, off, of one of the Villagers—the Cobbler—selling his wares

Cobbler (*off*) Boots for sale! Boots for sale! Finest shoes, clogs and boots for sale!

Puss looks up at Colin expectantly. Colin smiles and nods. Puss turns the page of the book back to the previous page:

SCENE 3

The exterior of the old mill

The Cobbler enters carrying a tray of boots, etc.

Cobbler Boots for sale!

Colin Here, Cobbler. How much are those little boots there?

Cobbler (*taking a small pair of boots from his tray*) One crown to you, sir.

Colin (*holding up the boots for Puss to see*) There, Puss. How would they be?

Puss shakes his head, and takes a pair of magnificent red, thigh-length boots off the tray

Good heavens, Puss. They'll cost the earth!

Cobbler Fine boots them, sir.

Colin How much?

Cobbler Fit for a prince!

Puss (*nodding in eager assent*) Miaow!

Cobbler They were made for a nobleman, but he never collected them.

Colin How much?

Cobbler Three crowns to you.

Colin You see, Puss? Too much! I only have one half-guinea piece in the world.

Cobbler Two and a half crowns!

Colin It's no good. I just haven't got it.

Cobbler All right, seeing it's you, Colin. Half a guinea!

Colin (*giving him the coin*) Oh well, there you are then.

Cobbler (*giving Puss the boots*) And there *you* are, Cat.

Puss hurriedly begins putting them on

Ha! A cat with boots! Now I've seen everything! Colin, lad, you must be mad. Ah well, there's one born every minute. Boots! Shoes! Boots for sale!

The Cobbler exits

There is a magic hiss of cymbals as Puss pulls on his boots

Colin You heard that, Puss? He thinks I'm mad! I think his judgement's——

Puss —rather sad!

Colin (*surprised*) Who said that? (*He looks around*) When I said "mad", someone said: "It's——

Puss —rather sad!

Colin Puss! That was you!

Puss   Of course it was; and now you'll see
                            The true worth of your half-guinea.
                            You bought the boots, but more than that,
                            You have bought a magic cat!

Colin Am I dreaming? Or *am* I going mad? I can hardly believe my ears? Puss, are you really a magic cat?

Puss   And clever too!
          Great fame and wealth, I'll bring to you.
          These boots will give me power unknown.
          May even lead me to a throne!
          But you must do just what I say.
          First fetch your things. We must away!

Colin (*in amazement*) Whatever you say, Master Puss!

Colin exits

Puss fetches a saucer of milk and puts it downstage to one side

Puss (*to the audience*)
          Now, children. Will you help me too?
          We have such dangerous things to do.
          If my ambition's to succeed,
          Then your assistance I shall need.
          This potion's of the strangest ilk,
          A saucerful of magic milk!
          And I shall need it for my friend
          'Ere this adventure has its end.
          But it's not safe, I know and feel it.
          Our enemies will try to steal it.
          But when they do—no matter how—
          Will you all cry: "Miaow!" "Miaow!"?
          Will you? . . . Come on. Let's have a go!
          Loudly now: Miaow! Miaow!
          (*He puts his paw to his ear*)

Audience Miaow!

Puss (*disappointedly*) Ooh!
          Come on! Get hep, cats! Make a row!
          Let's raise the roof! Miaow! Miaow!

Audience Miaow! Miaow!

Puss Again. Miaow!

Audience Miaow!

Puss   That's fine! Here comes that Cobbler now.
          So don't forget! Miaow! Miaow!

Puss exits

The Cobbler enters and sees the saucer of milk

Cobbler Ah! There's that stupid cat's milk. I think I'll have that just for a
joke. (*He goes to pick it up*)

Audience Miaow! Miaow!

*Puss rushes on and chases the Cobbler away. He waves to the audience in
triumph and exits*

*Gilbert and Filbert enter, leading a reluctant Oswald, the Ass, who is wearing
brown boots*

Gilbert (*pulling at Oswald's lead*) Did you hear them cats again?

Filbert (*pushing Oswald from behind*) Want a bucket of water over 'em. (*He looks at the audience*)
Gilbert Mangey beasts! Come on, Oswald, co-operate!
Filbert He doesn't like the ice.

Filbert suddenly slips through Oswald's rear legs and Oswald sits on his chest

Ohh! Oooh!

Gilbert Oswald! You silly ass! Get up! Get up!

Gilbert pulls with all his might on Oswald's lead. Oswald suddenly stands on his rear legs, Gilbert slips through his front legs and Oswald sits with his front legs on Gilbert's chest

OOOH! Help!
Filbert (*rising*) Ah, that's better!
Gilbert Help me, you fool.
Filbert Oh!

He pulls Oswald's tail. Oswald's front legs rise but Filbert slips through his rear legs again and Oswald is reseated on Filbert's chest

Oooh! Oooh!
Gilbert Come on, get up, you 'orrible brute.

Oswald rises suddenly and lurches forward, sitting again with his front legs on Gilbert's chest. Filbert is dragged along by the impact and Oswald reseats himself with his rear legs on Filbert's chest. Oswald is now sitting on Gilbert and Filbert

Get him off! Get him off!
Filbert Help! Help!
Gilbert Filbert, do something. Do something!
Filbert How can I?
Gilbert (*suddenly noticing that Oswald is wearing boots*) Hey, Filbert. Filbert! Filbert!
Filbert Yes? What is it?
Gilbert Why is this ass wearing brown boots?
Filbert His black ones are at the menders!

Oswald rises suddenly and moves away a little. Gilbert and Filbert also rise

I suppose this is how people get assma!
Gilbert (*looking at the audience*) It's sad, but it's true. Come on, you'd better get on him.
Filbert *Get* on him?
Gilbert Get on him.
Filbert *Me? On him?*
Gilbert *You*, on *him*. Go on. He's your ass.

Filbert crosses to Oswald's rear, but it is too high. He places one foot on top of his rump, but can't think how to get the other one up. Finally, he gives it up and replaces his foot on the ground

Filbert Will you give us a bunk up?

Gilbert Oh, spoilt! That's your trouble. Come on.

He stands to one side of Oswald and cups his hands. Filbert puts one foot in the cupped hands

One—two—three!

On "three", Filbert swings his other leg over Oswald's rear, but Oswald sits down on his rear legs and Filbert's leg continues on round and he finishes sitting astride Gilbert's shoulders

Come down! Come down this instance! You know, you try my patience.

Filbert descends. Oswald rises again

You'll have to take a run at him. When I count three. Ready?

Filbert (*gulping*) Yes.

Gilbert One—two—two and a half—three!

On "three" Filbert takes a running jump at Oswald's rear. But Oswald sits down again—this time front and back—and Filbert is left standing astride the collapsed ass

All right, Lester Piggott. Give it up.

Filbert turns round to watch him, still astride Oswald, but now facing the rear

(*Seeing the milk*) Hello, what's this? Milk? I could do with a drink. I'll pinch it.

Audience Miaow! Miaow!

Puss rushes on carrying a sack

Oswald rises with the terrified Filbert, seated on him back to front, and starts to canter off

Filbert (*as he goes*) Help! Put me down! Help! Gilbert! Help!

Oswald and Filbert exit

Gilbert Come back here, Filbert, stop showing off. Come back here.

He exits after them

Puss   Thank you, kids! The milk's still safe
From Gilbert and that other knave.
I yet may need its secret charm
To save my master's life from harm.
But now this sack's all I require
To seek the wealth of my young squire.
(*He turns two pages of the book*)
The next step to his fortune's made
When we have found the forest glade.
Ahhhhhhh! (*He purrs contentedly*)

He opens the page to:

SCENE 4

The forest

Puss exits stealthily

Music. The dancers enter wearing the head pieces and tails of various forest animals such as two rabbits, pheasant, deer, squirrel, fox, etc. and perform a ballet. They dance, play, chase each other, etc. Eventually, one of them finds the saucer of milk and they all gather round it to drink

Audience Miaow!

Puss enters with a large sack and the animals all disappear

Puss   What a lot of silly fauna!
                            But now a cunning plan I'm gonna
                            Execute, and fetch them back.
                            I need those idiots in my sack!

The music and ballet continue. Puss hangs his sack on a tree. The mouth hangs open, the end trails off, out of sight. He produces an old cuckoo-clock which he winds up

                            Curiosity—and simply that!—
                            You'll see, not only killed the cat!

He sets the clock going. It has a loud "tick-tock". He places it deep into the sack and then lies down, with the string attached to the neck of the sack in his hand. He pretends to go to sleep. The "tick-tock" continues loudly

One by one, the animals reappear. Cautiously, they approach the sack and peer in, listening to the noise. One by one, they enter the sack

When the last one is in, Puss pulls the string, which closes the neck of the sack tight. He takes it down from the tree, and drags it across the stage, now full of the shapes of the animals

                            Aha, my beauties! What a prize!
                            You'll make some lovely royal pies.
                            Off to the Queen now. That's the thing.
                            She'll make a dish fit for a king!
                            And put my master, with its flavour,
                            Right into the royal favour!

Puss exits

Gilbert and Filbert are heard, off. They are tired and irritable

Gilbert (*off*) Go *on*, Oswald! Giddyap!

There is the crack of a whip

(*Off*) Giddyap!

Filbert (*off*) Mush! Mush!

Gilbert enters leading Oswald, with Filbert bringing up the rear. Gilbert carries a whip and Filbert carries a small twig and they are both wearing swords

Gilbert (*cracking his whip*) Yeah! Yeah!
Filbert (*singing*) Yeah!

Filbert hits Oswald across the rump with his twig. Oswald kicks back at him and Filbert falls over backwards

Oswald wanders off

Gilbert All right, Wyatt Earp. How much wood have you got? (*He sits on the ground and begins to remove his boot*)

Filbert holds up his twig

Three hours in a forest, and that's all the wood you've collected?
Filbert Well I can't see the wood for the trees.

Gilbert removes his boot to reveal a sock which has a hole big enough to display three toes

Gilbert Oooh! That's better.
Filbert I say, look at your sock!
Gilbert That's all right. That's my atomic sock.
Filbert Atomic sock?
Gilbert Ninety per cent fall-out. (*He wiggles his toes*)
Filbert It's getting dark.
Gilbert (*replacing his boot*) Well, we'd better get on. We must find some firewood before sunset. It's dangerous here at night.
Filbert Oooh! That reminds me. (*He produces a box of powder, and proceeds to dance about, sprinkling the powder everywhere*)
Gilbert What *are* you doing? What's that?
Filbert (*sprinkling*) Elephant powder!
Gilbert *Elephant* powder?
Filbert (*sprinkling*) Elephant powder.
Gilbert Well I've never seen any elephants in this forest.
Filbert I know. Effective, isn't it? (*He sprinkles the powder*)
Gilbert Oh, you fool!
Filbert Pwhat, did you say?
Gilbert Fool!
Filbert So I'm a fool.
Gilbert You're a fool.
Filbert That's fighting talk.
Gilbert Fool!
Filbert Smile when you say that.
Gilbert (*smiling*) Fewl!
Filbert I don't like you talking to me like that. I've a good mind to let you have it.
Gilbert Why don't you?

Filbert I forgot where I put it.
Gilbert So?
Filbert Let's see the colour of your steel.
Gilbert The colour of my steel?
Filbert The colour of your steel.
Gilbert (*drawing his sword and pointing it at Filbert*) Now what?
Filbert Eh?
Gilbert (*brandishing his sword*) Now, what?
Filbert (*producing a pencil*) Will you sharpen my pencil, please?
Gilbert (*drawing Filbert's sword and shoving it into his hand; angrily*) Oh no
  you don't! I've had enough of your cheek. Here!
Filbert Oh!
Gilbert I don't like being made to look stupid.
Filbert Oh I shouldn't worry, it can't be helped!
Gilbert On guard!
Filbert On guard!
Gilbert Over here. Back to back.
Filbert Back to back.

They stand back to back C

Gilbert Now then, march! One. Two. Three. Four. Five. Six. Seven. Eight.
  Nine. Ten. Turn!

*Gilbert marches forward ten steps, but Filbert marches backwards ten steps, so
that they remain back to back, and when they turn, Filbert turns to the other
side of Gilbert, still remaining back to back, and Gilbert can't see him anywhere*

  Where are you? Where's he gone? Filbert! (*He finds him*) Over there! (*He
  points to the other side of the stage*)
Filbert Over there! (*He crosses to the other side of the stage*)
Gilbert On guard! (*He takes an exaggerated stance, and makes a short jump
  forward in the air*)
Filbert On guard! (*He does the same, and jumps forward*)
Gilbert On guard! (*He jumps again*)
Filbert ON GUARD! (*He jumps again*)
Gilbert On guard! (*He jumps to within striking distance of Filbert*)
Filbert On guard! (*He jumps on Gilbert's foot*)
Gilbert Oooh! (*He hops about holding his foot*)

*Suddenly the stage grows dark, and Blunderbore's voice is heard on the front-
of-house speakers as before*

Blunderbore (*off*) Hold it, mortals! Not so hasty!
                From here you two look rather tasty.
                I'm famished now. Forget your fight.
                You'll do for suppertime tonight.

  Oswald gallops in, terrified

  They all three stand quivering with fear C

And still the calories do come.
Another dish for my poor tum.
I can use that creature too,
In ass's milk to pickle you.

Gilbert (*on his knees*) Oh, please, Mr Ogre!
Filbert (*on his knees*) Don't eat us!

Oswald joins them on his knees, shaking and burying his head

Gilbert I'm allergic to pickle.
Filbert We'd curdle the milk.
Gilbert It brings me out in the most ghastly spots.
Filbert I'm terribly fattening!
Gilbert I'm horribly stringy!
Filbert }
Gilbert } (*together*) We're frightfully indigestible!

Blunderbore (*off*) I must have *someone* to eat I say!
            Why, dammit, I've not had a mortal all day!
Gilbert Well, why not try someone else? A little tastier!
Filbert (*standing*) Not quite so tough! (*He strikes his chest*)
Blunderbore (*off; roaring*) What?

Filbert falls down again

Gilbert What would you really like?
Filbert Yes! Really! Really!
Gilbert We'll gladly fetch it for you.
Blunderbore (*off*) Well let me see . . . I *really* would
            Enjoy a tasty royal pud!
Gilbert Royal pudding!
Filbert Royal pudding!
Gilbert Of course!
Filbert Lovely!
Gilbert Delicious!
Filbert All gooey and brown!
Gilbert And covered with custard!
Blunderbore (*off*) And made with royal blood!
Gilbert (*gulping*) Er—royal blood?
Blunderbore (*off*) The blood of a young princess!
Gilbert The blood of a young . . .
Blunderbore (*off*) Superb! So rare! So ex—qui—seete!
            Yes that would be a proper treat!
            A sweet princess, beg, steal, or borrow!
            And bring me her, by dusk tomorrow!

Gilbert and Filbert start to protest

            Do this at once! If not, then must
            I grind your feeble bones to dust!

A loud clap of thunder. Filbert covers his eyes, and shakes. The Lights come up

Filbert Has he gone?

Gilbert He's gone! But his tummy ain't 'arf rumbling!

Filbert What are we going to do?

Gilbert Well, it's quite simple. Either we kidnap a princess and have our heads chopped off, or we don't kidnap a princess and have our bones ground to dust.

Filbert Oh yes, it is simple isn't it? (*He pauses*) Which?

Gilbert Which? It's you that's simple. That's a magic ogre that is.

Filbert Magic ogre?

Gilbert He can turn himself into anything.

Filbert Turn himself into anything?

Gilbert Anything.

Filbert You mean like the milkman?

Gilbert The milkman? What's he got to do with it?

Filbert I've seen *him* turn his horse and cart into a sidestreet many a time!

Gilbert (*brandishing his sword*) I'll turn you into a pound of tripe in a minute. Now it shouldn't be hard to kidnap a princess.

Filbert You mean from the palace?

Gilbert They leave them all over the place.

Filbert The king will recognize us.

Gilbert Not him! He's too shortsighted. Anyway we'll disguise ourselves.

Filbert What as?

Gilbert Musicians! They're mad about music at the palace.

Filbert How will we get there?

Gilbert (*crossing to the seated Oswald*) We'll gallop there on Oswald. Come on, Oswald, on your feet.

Filbert and Gilbert attempt to raise Oswald, but his legs are still shaking frantically

Filbert I think he's still frightened.

Gilbert Come on, Oswald! Come on!

Oswald starts to collapse again

Filbert Giddyap! Giddyap!

Gilbert It's no good. I think we shall have to . . .

Filbert You don't mean . . .?

Gilbert Yes, I do . . .

They lift Oswald and start to carry him off

Filbert Couldn't we just walk?

Gilbert No. It's quicker by horse!

They exit

Puss enters and turns the page to:

SCENE 5

The royal palace

Puss exits

*Ferdy enters with his two daughters, the princesses Isabel and Rosalind.
Between them they carry a small spinet or harpsichord and a stool. Ferdy sits
and appears to play, Isabel turns the music and Rosalind sings a traditional
eighteenth-century air*

Song 6

Isabel Oh, Rosalind, that was beautiful. Your voice is fine and pure.

Ferdy Beautiful, daughter, beautiful! It reminds me of your mother's voice
  when I first knew her. Little flour!

Isabel Why did you call her "little flower", Papa?

Ferdy Well, she'd been through the mill, you know!

Rosalind In what way, Papa?

Ferdy Well, she'd lived a very sheltered life when I met her.

Isabel Sheltered?

Ferdy Horse shelters, bus shelters, air-raid shelters . . .

Isabel
Rosalind } (*together*) Oh, Papa!

Gerty enters, followed by Jack

Gerty Ferdy! Ferdy! Ah, there you are. Good. Now we can get on with our
  singing lesson. Jack, stand there. Have you got the music? Are you ready?

Ferdy (*sorting out his music*) Oh right deady, queerest!—er, queady rearest—
  er, yes!

Gerty (*snatching up a piece of music*) Have you been composing again?

Ferdy Oh, trust a jifle—er—a bit!

Gerty (*reading*) "The Second Movement"—"*From Not Paying Me Rent*"?

Ferdy A mere tagabelle!

Gerty (*returning the music*) Well, little things please little minds.

Ferdy (*absent-mindedly*) And little drawers fit little behinds.

Gerty *What* was that?

Ferdy Oh, ah—er—er . . .

Gerty Play!

Song 7

Ferdy plays and they all sing to the tune of "Frère Jacques"

All   What's for dinner? What's for dinner?
                           Irish stew, Irish stew!
                           Sloppy semolina, sloppy semolina!
                           No thank you! No thank you!

On the "you" note in the last line, Jack is hopelessly flat

Gerty (*speaking*) No, no, no! (*She strikes the note on the spinet. Singing*) "You!" "You!" "You!" "You!" Try it!
Jack (*singing*) "You."
Gerty Now then again!

They all sing it again. This time Ferdy is flat. They all look at him

Ferdy!
Ferdy Yes, dear?
Gerty Give me "A".
Ferdy Eh?
Gerty Give me "A".

Ferdy offers her a handful of straw

"A"! I want the key of "A"!

Ferdy removes one of the keys from the keyboard and hands it to her

Never mind! Here, let me have a bash.

Gerty turfs Ferdy out of his seat and sits

Now then again! (*She plays*)

They all sing "What's For Dinner". This time Ferdy and Jack are both flat

Oh, it's awful. I don't think either of you are breathing right. Breathe in!

Ferdy and Jack breathe in

Now out!

They breathe out

Deep breath. In! Hold it!

They breathe in and hold it

Isabel Mother!
Gerty Yes, dear?
Isabel Shouldn't those two beats be in the same bar?
Gerty If I catch either of 'em in the same bar, I'll slosh 'em with a shandy! Now where was I? Oh, yes. Again!

Gerty plays, and she, Isabel and Rosalind sing again, but Ferdy and Jack are still holding their breaths. As the song progresses they slowly become convulsed with the effort. The others finish the song, and Gerty suddenly notices Ferdy, red in the face and dancing about in agony

Ferdy! What are you doing?

They continue writhing

Ferdy! I will not have rock and roll in the palace! What's the matter with them?
Isabel You told them to hold their breaths.
Gerty Not for ever, you idiots. Give me strength. Breathe out!

Ferdy and Jack exhale and collapse. Isabel and Rosalind help them to sit up.

You'll do yourselves an injury, you will. You'd better have a drink. (*She sees the saucer of milk*) Here, this milk'll do.
Audience Miaow!

Puss enters, elegantly dressed, carrying his sack

Puss Your Majesties! (*He bows low*)
Gerty (*screaming*) Ahhh! What is it?
Rosalind It's all right, Mother. It's only a sweet little pussy cat.
Puss   My master greets Your Majesties;
                     And sends you gifts he hopes will please.
Gerty Gifts! On your feet, Ferdy. Yes? Do go on.
Ferdy Just a moment, young lady. Who *is* your master?
Jack Father! The "young lady" you're talking to is a cat.
Ferdy Well never mind. I'm sure she means well.
Gerty No, Ferdy dear. A gentleman cat.
Jack A tom. A tom.
Ferdy Oh, a nuclear cat. How very interesting.
Gerty (*with her eyes closed*) Why do we bother? What presents have you brought us, Cat?
Puss (*presenting her with the sack*)
                     My master sent all he was able,
                     Tender game for the royal table.
Gerty (*peering into the sack*) Oh I say, Ferdy, look here! (*She takes out the stuffed animals*) Pheasants, rabbits, venison—the lot!
Ferdy (*jocularly*) Well, well. That is a dishdy daint—a dashdy dint . . .
Gerty
Jack   } (*together*) Dainty Dish!
Isabel
Rosalind
Ferdy To bet before a sing—er—er—sing before a . . .
Gerty Give it up. Thank you, Cat. Very much.
Isabel Who is your master?
Puss   His loyal subjects know him as
                     The Lord Marquis of Carabas. (*He bows again*)
Jack (*mystified*) The Marquis of Carabas.
Gerty Well, it's very kind of him I'm sure.
Ferdy Yes, yes indeed.
Isabel Is he a young man?
Puss   Young, Your Highness, fair and strong.
                     He'll fight for right, but never do wrong.
Gerty Well, tell him, thank you very much.
Ferdy Yes, yes.
Isabel We'd like to meet him.
Ferdy Yes, yes.
Rosalind Tomorrow, at the royal hunt.
Gerty Well said, girls. So be it. Tell your master to meet us tomorrow in the forest for the royal hunt.

Puss On his behalf, I thank Your Majesty.

Gerty Now we'll just take this lot to the royal kitchen, and order lunch. Come, girls.

Isabel (*to Puss*) But don't go away.

Rosalind We will be back.

Gerty, Jack, Isabel and Rosalind exit, carrying the stuffed animals

Ferdy (*crossing to Puss and patting him on the head benevolently*) Good dog! Good dog!

Ferdy exits

Puss   My plan progresses. (*He looks off*) Who's outside? Gil, and Filbert! I must hide. (*He hides*)

Gilbert and Filbert enter, heavily disguised as musicians. Gilbert carries a cello, and Filbert a recorder

Gilbert Sssssssh!

Filbert Ssssssssh!

Gilbert A fine musician you look.

Filbert You're no Yehudi Manure.

Gilbert Have you got the score?

Filbert The score?

Gilbert The score!

Filbert Arsenal five—Chelsea nil.

Gilbert The music, you fool! (*He pulls it out of Filbert's pocket and hands it to him*) There!

Filbert Ah yes. Paganini.

Gilbert Paganini?

Filbert (*pointing to the music*) Paganini.

Gilbert (*looking at the music*) Page Nine! I dunno . . . Are you wearing that hat, or just walking underneath?

Filbert Everything's so tight. This collar is choking me.

Gilbert You've got your head through the buttonhole, you bert!

Filbert Oh it's hopeless. We'll never kidnap a princess like this.

Gilbert Now don't give up. We'll have to pass ourselves off as eccentric musicians.

Puss No.

Gilbert Eh?

Puss No you won't! (*He emerges*)

Gilbert Did you hear that?

Puss Your plot will fail.

Gilbert ⎫
Filbert ⎭ (*together*) It's Puss, the Cat!

Puss   Your plan's revealed. You've been betrayed. Within these walls a trap's been laid.

Gilbert   A trap?

Filbert   For us?

Gilbert
Filbert } (*together, to each other*) I told you so!

Puss   Fear not! A sure escape I know!
Gilbert   Escape?
                Oh, please!

Gilbert
Filbert } (*together*)   Oh, tell us how!

Puss (*holding up his sack*)
        You'll have to hide in here for now!
Gilbert   In that old sack?
Filbert   I wouldn't dare!
Puss   No-one will think to look in there.
        I'll say the sack is magic too.
        But all I tell them, you must do!
        Agreed?

Gilbert
Filbert } (*together*)   Agreed!

Puss   Now in you get!

Gilbert and Filbert climb into the sack. Puss hides their instruments

   (*Aside*)   Your evil plans you will regret.
            (*He ties the sack firmly at the neck*)
            Kidnap a princess?! I'll teach you yet
            A lesson you will not forget

Gerty, Ferdy, Jack, Isabel and Rosalind enter

Gerty Well, now we can get on with our singing lesson.
Isabel Well that's a bit hard on poor Puss.
Rosalind He deserves a reward, not a punishment.
Jack I hope his ears have strong resistance.
Puss Could I be of some assistance?
Jack The trouble is we all sing flat.
Puss   Oh, I've the perfect cure for that.
        The purest note you will get back
        If you simply kick this sack.
        Observe.

   (*He sings*)
"I love little Pussy, her coat is so——"

Puss kicks the sack. There is a short grunt followed by the voices of Gilbert and Filbert singing from the sack

Gilbert
Filbert } "—warm!"

Puss "And if I don't hurt her, she'll do me no——"

Puss kicks the sack and there is a grunt

Gilbert
Filbert } "—harm!"

Puss "I'll sit by the fire, and give her some——"

Puss kicks the sack and there is a grunt

Gilbert ⎫ "—food!"
Filbert ⎭

Puss "And she will love me if I'm gentle and——"

Puss kicks the sack and there is a grunt

Gilbert ⎫ "—good!"
Filbert ⎭

Gerty Wonderful! Wonderful! You see that Ferdy? A magic sack. It plays all the right notes. Now we can sing our song.
Ferdy Yes, dear.
Gerty Oh, goody gum-drops!
Jack May I try it?

Puss bows his assent. Jack gives the sack a tremendous kick

Gilbert ⎫ Ahhhhhhhh!
Filbert ⎭

Jack (*singing*) "Sweet mystery of life at last I've found you!" (*He kicks the sack again*)

Gilbert ⎫ Ohhhhhhhhh!
Filbert ⎭

Jack "At last I know the secret of it all!"
Gerty It's marvellous! Come on, kids, now. Gather round.

The others gather around the sack

Ready? Go!

All (*singing*)   "What's for dinner? What's for dinner?
                            Irish stew, Irish stew!
                            Sloppy semolina, sloppy semolina!
                            No thank——" (*They kick the sack*)

Gilbert ⎫   "—you!"
Filbert ⎭

All   "No thank——" (*They kick the sack*)

Gilbert ⎫   "—you!"
Filbert ⎭

They continue. Jack sings the first line solo, and one by one they join in, singing a round. Every time they reach "you" they kick the sack, leaving Gilbert and Filbert to sing. Soon this means that someone is kicking the sack every line. Eventually they finish. They congratulate each other, but then notice that piteous singing continues from the sack

Gilbert ⎫ "You! You! Youhoo! Yoooooooooooooooooh!"
Filbert ⎭

Gerty Sssh! Listen!

They look at the sack. It is shaking violently and moaning

Isabel Oh dear, something's wrong.
Jack I think we've broken it.
Rosalind What do we do now, Puss?
Puss   I think the sack has strained its throat.
                        We'd better throw it in the moat!

Even louder moans come from the sack

Isabel ⎫
Rosalind ⎭ (*together*) The moat?
Jack But won't that damage it, Puss?
Ferdy It'll get very damp.
Puss   No, no. It's hardly worth such bother.
                        I easily can make another!
Gerty Oh well, if you say so.
Jack All together!

Jack, Ferdy, Gerty and Puss start to lift the sack

Gerty Upsadaisy!
Puss   Into the moat! Out of the way!
                        This sack has really had its day!
                        All together heave!

Jack, Ferdy, Gerty and Puss exit with Gilbert and Filbert in the sack

Off, we hear the fading cries of Gilbert and Filbert as they descend into the moat, followed by a loud splash

Isabel and Rosalind exit, carrying the spinet and stool as Puss enters and turns the page back to:

Scene 6

The forest

Colin enters

Colin Puss! At last. I've been waiting for you for hours. Where have you been?
Puss   Making your fortune, never fear.
                        Their Majesties will soon be here.
Colin The King and Queen? Puss, what have you been up to?
Puss   All explanations later, pray.
                        For now, please do just what I say.
                        My cunning plan you will approve.
                        First all your clothes you must remove!
Colin Take my clothes off!
Puss   When I've a special signal made,
                        Jump in the lake, and cry for aid!
Colin Jump in the . . .! Puss, have you gone mad?

Puss   Will water harm you? Use your brain!
                    You've naught to lose, and all to gain.
Colin What can the *point* of all this be?
Puss   You'll benefit, I guarantee!
                    And what I ask is not so hard.
                    Quick now, undress, while I stand guard.

Puss exits

Colin (*beginning to undress*) I need my head examining. Taking orders from a cat.

Jill enters, carrying a bundle of wood

Jill Colin! Whatever are you doing?
Colin Oh, Jill! Er—just cooling off a bit.
Jill What in this weather?
Colin (*taking her bundle*) Can I take that for you?
Jill Oh, it doesn't matter. I'll just rest a bit. They're waiting for this at the camp.
Colin It must be fun living in a gypsy camp. I'd like to see it some day.
Jill Would you really, Colin? I would like to take you.
Colin What's it like to be a gypsy?
Jill We are a very proud people—like a little kingdom on our own.
Colin Kingdom?
Jill The forest is our kingdom.
Colin And you are the princess.
Jill Now you're making fun of me.
Colin No, Jill. You are just like a princess, in your forest. Beautiful and proud!
Jill Beautiful and proud! Why do you say such things—(*she snatches her bundle from him*)—when you don't mean them?
Colin But, Jill, I . . .
Jill Leave me alone! Aren't you ashamed—talking to a gypsy?
Colin Jill, I . . .
Jill Leave me alone!

Jill exits

Colin Well! There it is! A woman in love! She loves the Prince. The Prince loves her. So she pretends to be in love with me! And because I won't pretend to be in love with her, she's miserable! Why are people in love always so sad? That's not the way it's meant to be, I'm sure. (*He continues to remove his jacket and sings a love song*)

Song 8

Puss enters at the end of the song

Puss   Look out now—trouble! What still dressed?
                    You should be standing in your vest!
                    Run to the lake, at a sign from me,
                    You shout for help as loud can be!

Puss and Colin exit

Gilbert and Filbert enter, disguised as a couple of rather old trees. All we can see of them is their faces poking through two single holes in the trunks, and their feet. Their arms appear to be branches

Filbert It'll never work.

Gilbert Of course it will. Don't be such an old slobber chops!

Filbert Don't you call *me* names. Bean pole!

Gilbert I *beg* your pardon? Don't talk to me like that, just 'cos I can't get at you, you freckle-faced faggot!

Filbert It was your fault we got chucked in the moat. Clodpole!

Gilbert Oh yes, that's right, blame me. Bacon Bonce!

Filbert Six feet two and a tea-leaf!

Gilbert Selfish little horror!

Filbert   Gilbert is kind, and Gilbert is strong.
                    Gilbert is nice, but he don't half——

Gilbert Filbert! Shut your mouth!

Filbert Shut your own, it's closer!

Gilbert (*waddling with difficulty towards Filbert*) You wait! Till I get out of this. I'll separate you from your breath.

Filbert Here just a minute. Is your hair wet?

Gilbert No, why?

Filbert There's a big drip under it! (*Delighted with himself*) Ha! Ha! Ha!

A trumpet sounds, far off

Gilbert Sssh! Quiet! Listen! (*He pauses*) It's them!

Filbert They!

Gilbert Oh, hold your clack!

Filbert Wrap up and wind your neck in!

Gilbert Now listen. This is the plan.

Filbert I'm all ears!

Gilbert Well never mind, that's not your fault. We stand here, pretending to be trees. As soon as a princess passes, I grab her. You cover the rear. If there's any trouble, fire at will!

Filbert How am I going to tell which one is Will with all them people?

Gilbert Look out! There's someone coming!

They take up their attitudes as trees, to one side of the stage

A powerful-looking Woodcutter enters, carrying a large axe, looking for suitable trees

He looks around the stage, and his eyes come to rest on Filbert, on the far side of Gilbert. His eyes light up contentedly

Woodcutter Ah!

He crosses Gilbert, to the other side of Filbert, leans his axe against Filbert, and spits on his hands. He takes up the axe, and tests the blade with his thumb. Filbert taps the Woodman on his shoulder, furthest away from himself. The

Woodman turns to look, and Filbert runs round to the other side of Gilbert. The Woodman looks back, and is surprised to find Filbert gone. He passes it off, and takes a few practice swings with his axe beside Gilbert. Gilbert taps the Woodman's shoulder. Again he looks round, and Gilbert runs to the other side of Filbert. The Woodman looks back again, and is bewildered. He crosses to Filbert, measures up to him, and again does a few practice swings. Filbert taps him on the shoulder. The Woodman swings round angrily, finds nobody, and scratches his head in dismay. Filbert runs round Gilbert, who runs round Filbert. The Woodman looks back, and is amazed. They are nearly the other side of the stage! A cunning expression comes over his face, and he nods to himself slyly. He crosses and stands between them! Again he prepares himself, to chop down Filbert. Gilbert taps his shoulder. He swings round to look at Gilbert, and Filbert runs round them both to the other side of Gilbert. The Woodman looks back to where Filbert was—he is gone! He looks at the audience in astonishment. Both Gilbert and Filbert run round behind the Woodman to the other side of him (Filbert in his original position beside him). The Woodman looks back for Gilbert—he is gone! He looks again at Filbert— he is back! He looks at the audience in anguish

> *Filbert runs round Gilbert, who runs round Filbert, who runs round Gilbert, etc., etc., until they exit*

The Woodman rubs his eyes, then he looks left and right, and all round him

> *He bursts into tears and exits*

Quick pause

> *Gilbert and Filbert creep back on again*

Filbert Well, of course, you're determined to get me killed, aren't you?
Gilbert Well, how was I to know?
Filbert I've no desire to end up as a box of matches, thank you very much!
Gilbert Phoo! I've had it! I'm dying of thirst.
Filbert Me too.
Gilbert Oh look, there's that saucer of milk again. Let's 'ave a swig of that.

They approach the milk

Audience Miaow!

> *Puss enters with a dog (real if possible) on a lead, and approaches them*

Gilbert (*seeing the dog*) Oh, no! No! Not that! Help!

> *Gilbert and Filbert exit in panic. Puss and the dog follow them off*

There is a fanfare of trumpets

> *The royal hunting party, consisting of Ferdy, Gerty, Jack, Isabel, Rosalind and Attendants, enter. They carry spears and various hunting weapons. Ferdy has discarded his crown and now wears a sou'wester back to front*

Gerty Well, this is where we arranged to meet the Marquis of—— what was it?

Isabel Carabas!

Gerty suddenly slaps the back of her neck

Gerty Drat the things!

Jack Mosquitoes, Mater?

Gerty Trouble with me—too much insex appeal! (*To Ferdy*) 'Ere you!

Ferdy Yes, dear?

Gerty Why are you wearing your sou'wester back to front?

Ferdy There's a nor'wester blowing!

Gerty Of course I had to ask.

Jack Seen any boar yet, Mater?

Gerty Only your father.

Colin (*off*) Help! Help! I'm drowning! Help!

   Puss enters

Puss (*bowing low*)
        Your Majesties! Such dire distress!
        My master's robbed of all his dress!
        What's more, the thieves his life would take!
        And flung him headlong in the lake!

Isabel   The lake!

Gerty   Poor Marquis!

Jack   The rotten swine!

Ferdy   How many thieves?

Puss   Some eight or nine!

Gerty (*to Jack and the Attendants*)
        Well help—at once! Before he's dead!

Jack   Where *are* the thieves? (*He begins to go*)

Puss (*following him and the Attendants*)
        They are all fled!

   Jack, the Attendants and Puss exit

Isabel But in this cold the marquis will catch pneumonia!

Gerty Better send for the undertaker!

Rosalind Don't you mean the doctor?

Gerty I never deal with middlemen!

   Puss, Jack and the Attendants enter with Colin, who is wrapped in a large cloak

Puss May I present, Your Majesties, the Lord Marquis of Carabas!

Colin (*astonished*) Marquis? . . . Puss . . . I . . .

Gerty I know your face! I've seen it before! Didn't we meet once at Olney?

Colin I've never been to Olney, Your Majesty!

Gerty No. Neither have I. It must have been two other people. This is the King, my husband, Ferdinand.

Colin Your Majesty!

Ferdy (*shaking hands*) Oh how do you do, Ferdinand.

Gerty (*to Colin*) Ignore it. The Prince you've met. These are my daughters. Rosalind.

Colin Your Highness.
Rosalind Marquis.
Gerty And Isabel, the youngest.
Colin Your Highness.
Isabel Marquis.

Their eyes meet—and they fall in love. The orchestra plays gently a few bars of Song 8

Gerty (*watching Colin and Isabel for a moment*) Yes. Well, you can have another look in a minute. (*To the Attendants*) First, build a large fire, and send for clothes—royal clothes—worthy of a handsome marquis!
Attendant Yes, Your Majesty!

The Attendants exit

Gerty Come, sir! Sir?

Colin comes to and turns to Gerty

What are your political affiliations, Marquis?
Colin I really don't know, Your Majesty. I suppose I must be a liberal.
Gerty I belong to the Liberal Party, *and* the Conservative Party, *and* the Labour Party.
Colin Your Majesty is fond of politics?
Gerty Can't bear them. But I *love* parties!

Gerty, Colin, Puss, Jack and Ferdy exit

Isabel Oh, Rosalind! How handsome he is!
Rosalind Yes, sister.
Isabel He's beautiful.
Rosalind Yes, sister.
Isabel Rosalind, I believe I—I don't know, I—I believe I . . .
Rosalind Yes, Isabel. I know.
Isabel Can it be love—so quickly?
Rosalind Who knows? We shall see.
Isabel Oh, Rosalind, I feel wonderful! Wonderful!
Rosalind Certainly that is a symptom.
Isabel Rosalind, why have you never fallen in love?
Rosalind I can tell you the reason, but you may not understand it. There is a strange twilight envelopes my spirit. Nearly dark, almost beautiful. For many years it has haunted me, bidding me . . . wait. Listen, sister, I will tell you. (*She sings a love song*)

Song 9

Gilbert and Filbert, normally dressed, creep in quickly at the end of the song

Gilbert seizes Isabel and makes off with her, his hand clasped over her mouth

Rosalind Help! Help! Robbers! Help! Murder! Ho! Jack! Guards! Help!

Filbert struggles with her

Filbert (*as he does so*) Sssh! Now stop it. Hold your noise, miss. Quiet! Sssh! Can it, can't you! Hush! Hush!

He finally succeeds in throwing her to the ground and hurries off after Gilbert

We hear horses galloping away

Rosalind Help! Please someone! Help!

Jill enters, and runs to Rosalind's aid

Jill Your Highness! What is it?

Rosalind They've . . . taken . . . Isabel . . . stolen . . . horses . . . (*She faints*)

Colin enters, magnificently dressed as a courtier. He wears a sword

Colin What is it?

Jill Colin!

Colin Ssh! (*Whispering*) Marquis! What's happened?

Jill Princess Isabel has been kidnapped. They seem to have taken her off towards the Ogre's castle! But what . . .?

Colin Tell the others! Don't betray me! (*He draws his sword*) I'm going after them!

Colin exits

Gerty, Ferdy and Jack enter

Gerty Oh my heavens! Whatever is it? (*She goes to aid Rosalind*)

Jill It's Princess Isabel, Your Majesty. She's been captured and taken to the Ogre's castle. Col—— I mean the Marquis has gone after them.

Jack Will he catch them?

Jill Never. They have stolen the royal horses. He'll never save her alone. The Ogre's castle is guarded like a fortress!

Gerty The Ogre will never let her go. *He*'s so mean, he wouldn't even spend Christmas! (*She weeps*)

Jack I'm going after him! (*He starts to go*)

Jill No! Jack!

Jack What is it?

Jill I . . . take care! I . . . will be waiting!

Jack stares at her for a moment, smiles and exits

Gerty Ferdy! Don't just stand there! Do something, you ninny!

Ferdy Yes, of course, dear! Of course. We must be rough and toothless—er—tough and ruthless! (*He draws his tiny sword, and runs after Jack*) Jack! Wait for me! Wait!

Ferdy exits

Rosalind (*coming to*) Where am I? Mother!

Gerty There, there, dear. Don't worry.

Jill I will take her to my camp till she is stronger.

Rosalind Is Isabel . . .?

Jill They've gone to save her.

Gerty Where's Ferdy?
Jill He went after the others.
Gerty *What?* Oh no! Not Ferdy! He mustn't! He'll get hurt! He can't tell an ogre from an orange. (*She runs after Ferdy*) Ferdy! Come back! Ferdy!

Gerty exits

Jill Come, Your Highness. I will take care of you till they return.

They cross to the exit. The refrain of Song 8 begins softly

Rosalind My poor sister. (*After a pause*) And brother Jack.
Jill He is brave.
Rosalind You love him, don't you, Jill?
Jill I love him.

They exit

The music continues

Puss enters. He wears a sword

Puss   A pandemonium I heard,
                But what has happened? Not a word!
                They've disappeared. So all's not well.
                But is there no-one here to tell?

Oswald enters, very agitated

(*Seeing Oswald*) Ah!

Oswald gallops across to Puss and whispers excitedly in his hear

(*Listening*)
                Villains! Rogues! They should be quartered.
                What? . . . Fools? . . . They'll all be slaughtered.
                This problem needs a feline guile;
                Wit, cunning and a certain style!

He leaps on to Oswald's back and draws his sword. Oswald circles the stage

                I'll trounce that Ogre till he hoots.
                He'll be no match for Puss in Boots!

They gallop off

The music swells up triumphantly as——

—*the* CURTAIN *falls*

ACT II

SCENE 1

A haunted corridor in the Ogre's castle

The book is open to represent a corridor. There is a large, free-standing, ornamental clock C, with a large bell in front. Downstage to one side, there is a large, full-length, glassless mirrorframe and a large laundry basket

As the CURTAIN *rises weird, ghostly music, full of creaks and wind and whistles, is playing*

A Ghost enters, like a long sheet with eyes. He crosses the stage and exits. Another Ghost, similarly dressed, but carrying a monstrous ball and chain attached to his leg, limps across the stage and exits. Two other Ghosts enter, one wearing a hat. They meet C. *The one Ghost raises his hat and bows, the other raises his head and bows. They exit*

The music changes to the song for the Ghost number

A line of Ghosts enters, followed by a sort of Sergeant Ghost. They all march up and down the corridor and sing

Song 10

The Ghosts march off at the end of the song

Gerty, Jack and Ferdy creep on very carefully

They are just C *when there is a very loud rattling clockwork sound from the clock. They hide behind the laundry basket and watch*

From behind the clock two enormous mechanical figures appear—Father Time and Cupid. They travel round to the bell, and strike the half-hour. It is half-past eleven. They turn jerkily and travel back to behind the clock

Gerty I thought it was Liberace and his agent! Look out!

Two Ghosts sweep across the stage and exit

Jack Late for choir practice!

Gerty, Jack and Ferdy emerge from behind the laundry basket

Ferdy I don't think the Ogre will be very pleased to see us.
Gerty I don't care. I'm going to have it out with old Rumble Tummy once and for all. He's not going to pinch my kids and get away with it. It's the biggest daylight robbery since United Counties put up the bus fares! (*She opens the laundry basket and holds up a sheet*)

Jack Well, I think it would be better if we rescued Isabel without meeting the Ogre.

Ferdy Yes, he does eat people so! He must be this hungry young man we're always hearing about.

Gerty Isn't he marvellous?

Jack Look out! Here comes another!

He and Ferdy dash behind the clock

Gerty throws the sheet over her head, which makes her look like a ghost, and stands behind the mirror

The Ghost enters

He looks at the clock, then he crosses and looks at himself in the mirror—only of course it is Gerty he is staring at. He cocks his head to one side—so does Gerty. He straightens it—so does she. Something is not quite right! He turns sideways—Gerty turns sideways. He turns to the front again—so does Gerty. He turns sideways the other way—so does Gerty. He turns with his back to the mirror and peers over one shoulder—so does Gerty. He comes back to the front of the mirror and peers at himself so closely that their noses touch. Slowly they go round in a complete circle, nose to nose. He steps into the mirror—she steps out. He steps out of the mirror—she steps in again. The Ghost apparently gives it up and turns his back on the mirror, but suddenly swings back—so does Gerty. He waves goodbye, still a trifle suspicious—so does Gerty. He turns to the clock and compares it with his own: a sundial on a chain. The clock is slow and he turns the hand to midnight

The Ghost exits

Ferdy and Jack appear instead of the mechanical figures, Ferdy in his vest and pants as Cupid and Jack, with a long beard, as Father Time. They both carry hammers

They shuttle round to the bell, strike the hour chimes and then twelve strokes of midnight. At the eleventh stroke Ferdy collapses exhausted over the bell and Jack's hammer comes down on his head and knocks him out on twelve

Gerty You clumsy clot! Look what you've done!

Jack turns to look at Gerty who is still dressed as a ghost, and screams in terror

(*Removing the headpiece*) It's all right. It's only me! Come on. Let's bring his nibs round. (*She slaps Ferdy's wrist, etc.*) Come on Ferdy, ease up!

Ferdy (*coming to*) Tea's up? Where? Where?

Gerty Now don't be greedy. You had a dirty great cupful during the interval.

Ferdy What happened?

Gerty You was counted out. Come on, on your feet! (*She crosses to the laundry basket, and hands them sheets*) And get into these.

Jack (*taking the sheet*) What for?

Gerty We're going to disguise ourselves as three of the Ogre's ghosts.

Ferdy (*putting on his sheet*) I've always fancied myself as a vision.

Gerty Well, you've been giving me the willies for years.

Jack (*parading himself*) How's that?

Gerty More like the back door than Christian Dior, but it'll do.

Ferdy And me, dear?

Gerty You look like an unmade bed! Close the basket.

Ferdy starts to do so

(*Whispering*) Now we mustn't make any noise.

Jack (*whispering*) No noise!

Ferdy (*whispering*) No noise! (*He drops the laundry basket lid on to his hand and yells with pain*) Ohh!

Gerty (*loudly*) Quiet!

Jack Ssssh!

Ferdy Ssssh!

Gerty Ssssh! (*She sings*)

Song 11. We Must Be Ever So Quiet

This is a full house number, during which the tabs close behind Gerty, Jack and Ferdy, cutting off the rear half of the stage to facilitate a quick change to the next scene. At the end of the house number Jack hears someone coming

Jack Look out! They're coming back!

Ferdy Hide.

Gerty Our big opportunity!

Jack
Ferdy } (*together*) Quiet! Sssh!

Gerty, Jack and Ferdy hide behind the laundry basket

The Ghosts enter in single file and stop

The Sergeant Ghost walks along the line, counting them in silence. At the end he has started from, Gerty, Jack and Ferdy join the line. At the other end of the line the Sergeant turns round and sees the longer line. Bewildered, he starts from that end and counts again. Gerty, Jack and Ferdy run round to the other end. The Sergeant reaches the opposite end. The number is right! He looks along the line again, but it still looks too big. He counts again and Gerty, Jack and Ferdy run round the back again. The Sergeant reaches the other end and looks back. He is still not convinced and counts again very quickly. Gerty, Jack and Ferdy run round the back, but this time Gerty loses her headpiece and her face is exposed. She does not notice this and stands next to the last real Ghost at her end, smiling happily

The Sergeant, fed up, throws up his hands and exits

The others stand there in a line. Jack nudges Gerty and tries to draw her attention, but she ignores him. The end Ghost turns, sees Gerty's face, does a double-take, and shakes with terror

The end Ghost looks again and runs off in horror

Gerty moves up a place. Ferdy and Jack follow suit

*The next Ghost turns, sees Gerty, and exits in terror. This goes on all down
the line until all the Ghosts have gone leaving Gerty, Jack and Ferdy*

Ferdy and Jack remove their headpieces

Jack Well that was a great success.
Gerty Really, what a shaky lot!
Jack Well, Mater, your headpiece is missing.
Gerty What? You mean they saw my face?
Ferdy It scared the wits out of them, my dear!
Gerty I don't want any of that!

A loud alarm bell sounds

What's that?
Ferdy Tea break.
Jack Something's up.

*Jack and Ferdy leap behind the laundry basket and Blunderbore's voice is heard
via offstage speakers*

Blunderbore (*off*) You! Who *are* you? How d'you dare
                        To infiltrate my castle lair?

A loud gong sounds

The Ogre's Guards (masked with "monkey faces") enter, carrying swords

*Gerty, Jack and Ferdy are suddenly surrounded by the Guards and a circle of
gleaming swords*

                        Seize them, men! Straight to the kitchen.
                        Now for my royal dish I'm itchin'.
                        Of ingredients there's no dearth.
                        I'll cook the biggest pud on earth!
                        Ha! Ha! Ha! Ha!

The Guards march Gerty, Jack and Ferdy off to the kitchen

Colin enters stealthily, watching where the others have been led off

Quick pause

Puss enters

Colin So you're here, Puss. I might have known.
Puss   Master! Won't you please go home?
                      The situation's not so tragic.
                      It just requires a touch of magic.
                      With cunning I shall win the day,
                      So don't you see, you're in the way?
Colin Thank you, Puss, but I shall stay!
Puss   Oh, very well, just as you say.
                      But if you do, be ruled by me.
                      Conform to my sagacity.
                      Obey my orders, understand?
                      Then we shall win!

Colin (*bowing*) At your command.

> *Two masked Guards, armed with swords, enter and creep towards Colin from behind him*

Puss   Our plan of campaign's not too hard ...
(*He sees the Guards*)
Look out, Master! Quick! On Guard!

Colin swings to one side, just as the Guards rush him. He trips one, draws his sword, and engages with the other. Puss draws his sword and engages with the tripped Guard. After a short fight they defeat the Guards

          Good work! We soundly cooked their pigeon!
          And now, next stop, the Ogre's kitchen!

   Colin exits

Puss appears to pull back the tabs to disclose:

Scene 2

The Ogre's kitchen

Puss and the Guards exit

The book is open to represent the Ogre's kitchen. To one side of the stage is a solid flat to which is attached rungs (unseen by the audience) for when Puss has to "run up the wall" later in the scene. There is a giant table c and sitting behind it, on a giant chair, is Blunderbore, the Ogre. This is achieved by the actor (or actress) standing on the chair, under a giant head, and wearing clothes to represent the top half of Blunderbore—his arms being extended with the aid of two sticks. We see only down as far as Blunderbore's waist—i.e. the actor's feet—as a tablecloth covers the side of the table facing the audience. On the table in front of Blunderbore there is a giant knife and fork, a plate and a cup. The cup has a hole in the bottom, so that the monkey hides beneath the table and appears as if from inside the cup later in the scene. To one side of the stage is a large oven, which is attached by nylon thread to the flies. On the other side, in tall cages into which they just fit, are Gerty, Ferdy and Jack. There is a Guard either side of the three cages

Blunderbore's voice is heard via onstage speakers

Blunderbore   Well, my beauties, here we all are!
Welcome, to my coffee bar!
"Ogie's Place", where the élite do meet,
To wine and dine on human meat.
What's on the menu?
Guard Consommé of ground prince.
Blunderbore Ahh!
Jack Oh!

Guard Fried Ferdinand and chips.
Blunderbore Ahh!
Ferdy Oh!
Guard Steak and Gerty pie.
Blunderbore Ahh!
Gerty Oh!
Guard And the pudding . . .
Blunderbore (*in ecstacy*) Don't tell me! Don't tell me!

Silence

Well? Go on, tell me!
Guard Royal pudding!
Blunderbore (*nirvana*) Royal pudding!
Guard Made from genuine princess with blue-blooded sauce!
Gerty
Ferdy } (*together*) Oh!
Jack
Blunderbore Divine!
Gerty
Ferdy } (*together*) Oh!
Jack
Blunderbore Superb! (*He sings*)

Song 12. Hokey Pokey

> King porridge hot,
> Queen porridge cold,
> Prince porridge in the pot
> Nine days old.
>
> Some like 'em raw,
> Some like 'em peeled,
> Some like 'em in the pot
> Nicely grilled.
>
> But—
>   Hokey, pokey, whiskey, thum,
>   How dw'I like princesses done?
>   Boiled in whiskey, boiled in rum,
>   Boiled in the blood of their father and mum.

Jack But look here, old boy——
Blunderbore (*speaking*) Quiet! Not finished yet! (*He sings*)
>   An Ogre called Horner
>   Sat in the corner,
>   Eating his Christmas pie;
>   Instead of a plum
>   He pulled out a thumb,
>   And said what a good boy am I!
>
> Hee hee hee ha ha ha haw haw haw!

Hokey, pokey, whiskey, thum,
How dw'I like princesses done?
Boiled in whiskey, boiled in rum,
Boiled in the blood of their father and mum.

(*Speaking*) One more time—(*He sings*)
Old King Cole
Served up like sole,
With a dainty mashed marquis,
With duchess's girls
And jellied earls,
And a bombay duke for tea.

(*Speaking*) All together now—(*He sings gaily*)
Hokey, pokey, whiskey, thum,

The others sing miserably with Blunderbore

Blunderbore
Gerty　　　How dw'I (Howd's he) like princesses done?
Jack　　　　Boiled in whiskey, boiled in rum,
Ferdy　　　Boiled in the blood of their father and mum.

Gerty Oh, Sir Blunderbore, spare us! Spare us!

Ferdy
Jack } (*together*) Spare us!

Jack Sir Blunderbore, might I make a suggestion?

Blunderbore Hmm?

Jack My mother is the Queen of Hearts.

Blunderbore So?

Jack She's known all over the world for her famous tarts.

Blunderbore (*dubiously*) And?

Jack You know: (*he sings nervously*) "The Queen of Hearts, she made some tarts, all on a summer's day."

Blunderbore No!

Gerty Well, he's doing his best!
It's so dark down here. I'm all of a shiver.
Where are your lights?

Blunderbore　　　　　　　　　　　Next to me liver!
(*He roars with laughter*)

Jack What I was going to say, sir, as she makes such delicious tarts, it seems such a frightful waste to eat her, and not her tarts, if you see what I mean, sir.

Gerty Now, Jack, now steady! Don't be hasty!

Blunderbore These tarts, are they so very tasty?

Jack Divine!

Ferdy 　　　Superb!

Jack 　　　　　　You'd love them too!

Blunderbore All right. I'll tell you what I'll do.
Before each meal, a nap I take.
You make the tarts before I wake.

A Guard approaches Blunderbore with a large handkerchief

> Release them, Guards, and hither bring
> The milk and flour and everything.
> If good as they're supposed to be,
> *Perhaps*, I'll set your Princess free.

Gerty And me? I baked them after all!
Blunderbore You'll stay!—as Cook! Well, good-night all!

The Guard covers Blunderbore's head with the handkerchief and he falls asleep

The Guard exits

Meanwhile the other Guard releases Ferdy, Gerty and Jack from their cages

The other Guard exits with the cages

Gerty Well that was a great help!
Jack At least we gained a little time!
Gerty But I've never so much as cooked an egg in me life!
Jack But—but, Mater. That famous old rhyme about the tarts?
Gerty Apocryphal, my dear boy.
Jack Oh! What does that mean?
Gerty We're up the creek! (*To Ferdy*) You! Think of something!

But nothing is forthcoming

> Silence reigned, and we all got wet!

Jack I say, Mater, you don't think the Ogre would marry Isabel, for half your kingdom or something, instead of eating her?
Ferdy That's an excellent suggestion, my dear. What they call a marriage in the convenience.

The Guards return with a large trolley on which are a pile of about a dozen metal plates, a large jar of yeast, a bowl, a strong paper bag containing flour, and two soda syphons

Jack Here come the utensils, Mater.
Gerty Yes, well we'd better get crackin'. What do you do first?
Ferdy You knead the dough.
Gerty Come again?
Ferdy You knead the dough.
Gerty I've always needed the dough, but you never give it to me!

Jack pours flour into the bowl, then bangs the empty bag. The surplus flour blows into Gerty's face. She snatches the bag from him

> Don't do that!

Jack What?
Gerty That! (*She bangs the bag of flour and blows it into Jack's face*)
Ferdy What's that, dear?
Gerty That! (*She bangs the bag into Ferdy's face*)
Jack (*taking up a syphon*) Now, put in some water!

He fires the syphon which rebounds off the bowl on to Gerty

Gerty Don't do that! (*She snatches up the other syphon and fires it at Jack*)
Jack Well, really!

He fires again at Gerty, but she ducks and he hits Ferdy full in the face

Gerty Now what?
Jack Mix it!
Ferdy Knead the dough!
Gerty You'll need an ambulance if you don't give over. You two mix it while
    I sort out these plates.

*Ferdy and Jack mix the pastry. Gerty goes round to below the trolley, picks up
the pile of plates and throws them on to the floor one after the other with a
clatter. At round about number ten—which is a cardboard plate—she takes a
quick look at the plate, then flings it out into the audience. She finishes, puts the
plates back on the trolley and rejoins Ferdy and Jack*

    They seem all right. How are you doing?
Jack (*with his hands in the bowl*) Oooh! Oh, I'm stuck!
Gerty What do you mean, stuck?
Jack I can't seem to get my hands out.
Gerty Don't panic. I'll grab your waist and pull you out. (*She grabs his waist*)
    Ferdy, you grab the top of the bowl. When I nod my head, push it.
Ferdy Eh?
Gerty When I nod my head, push it.
Ferdy If you say so, dear.
Gerty Right—now! (*She nods*)

*Ferdy pushes her head. As his hands are covered with dough, he leaves a hefty
deposit on the side of her face*

    Don't do that!

*She grabs a handful of dough and pushes it into Ferdy's face. He runs round to
the other side of Jack. Suddenly, Jack, who has been tugging and pulling all this
time, frees himself and his arms shoot out of the bowl hitting Ferdy and Gerty,
who are either side of him, in the face with more dough*

Gerty |
Ferdy | (*together*) Don't do that!

*They stick some more dough on Jack's face and then they put all the loose dough
back in the bowl*

Gerty For heaven's sake, let's get on with these tarts. What's next?
Jack Put some on a plate, flatten it, leave it to stand, then bung it in the oven.
Gerty (*putting a dollop on a plate*) Put some on a plate. Flatten it. (*She bashes
    the dollop flat*) Leave it to stand. (*She puts the plate on Blunderbore's table*)
    We'll leave it there until we've made the next one. Then we'll bung 'em both
    in the oven.

*During the following, a Monkey appears from inside Blunderbore's cup, steals
the plate and disappears back into the cup*

Put some on a plate. (*She does so*) Flatten it. (*She does so*) Leave it to stand. (*She takes the second plate to Blunderbore's table and discovers the first one is missing*) Here! Who's pinched me tart? (*She puts the plate on the table*) Jack! Have you been up to your tricks again?

The Monkey appears again, takes the second plate and disappears back into the cup

Jack No, Mater! No! You remember, you said that old story was a pocketful.
Gerty I don't want any excuses. Ferdy! What do you know about that tart?
Ferdy Well, my dear, you have to knead the dough.
Gerty What I need is a rolling pin, to bash your bonce. Well, we'll have to make another.

The others watch her

Put some on a plate. (*She does so*) Flatten it. (*She does so*) Leave it to stand. (*She takes the plate to Blunderbore's table*) Here! Now the other one's gone! (*She puts the third plate on the table and turns to Jack*) You little wretch!

She starts to chase him round the table, trying to hit him

Jack It wasn't me, Mater! It must have been Pater!

He chases Ferdy and they all three circuit the table two or three times, during which, of course, the Monkey removes the third plate

There look, that one's gone too! And it wasn't me!
Ferdy And it wasn't me!
Gerty Well all right! All right! I'll make one more! And this time I won't take me eyes off it. (*She takes out the tiny morsel of dough that is left*)
Jack He'll need a magnifying-glass to see that.
Gerty Is that all there is left?
Jack (*picking up the flour bag*) Well see for yourself, there's no more flour. (*He bangs the bag and the flour blows in Gerty's face again*)
Gerty Don't do that! (*She snatches the bag and hits his head with it*) Well, we'll have to try it. Put it in the plate. (*She does so*) Flatten it! (*She does so*) We will *not* leave it to stand. We will put it straight in the oven. (*She opens the oven door, and puts the plate in*)
Jack (*taking up the giant jar of yeast*) I know! Put some yeast in. That might make it rise.
Gerty Good idea.
Jack How much?
Gerty Here! Bung the lot in. (*She puts the yeast in the oven and closes the door*) Now, switch on. And hope for the best!

Jack switches on the oven. There is a hissing noise and they all watch. Slowly, to the music of "Thus Spake Zarathustra" by Strauss, the whole oven rises and disappears through the ceiling

Jack Well it rose all right.

Two Guards enter. One removes the handkerchief from Blunderbore's head

Gerty Look out! It's the fuzz!

Jack Looks as if our time is up!

Blunderbore (*waking up and yawning*) Ahhhhrrr!
               I had a pleasant forty winks! (*He sniffs*)
               Hello! There's something round here stinks!
               It's supper time! I quite forgot!
               Those tarts must now be nice and hot!

Gerty The tarts, well—as a matter of fact—they . . .

Blunderbore Yes?

Gerty (*gulping*) Disappeared!

Blunderbore Disappeared?

Gerty Disappeared!

Blunderbore (*sweetly*)
               Well don't worry. Never mind.
               We all make errors of that kind.
               I understand. My tarts you spoil.
               It's quite all right. (*Yelling*) Boil her in oil!

Gerty Oh!

Blunderbore (*in a fury*)
               You couldn't make an Irish stew!
               Seize them! We'll have no more to do!

The Guards seize them

               Now! On with supper. Bring the gel!
               I'll start by eating Isabel!

Two other Guards bring in Isabel, chained. They then wheel off the trolley

               Ah, there she is! I'm sure *this* dish is
               Going to taste simply delicious!

Isabel Mother! Jack!

Gerty Isabel! My baby! (*She weeps*)

Blunderbore Now stop that din! She's not cooked yet.
               Guards make sure the oven's set.
               But where's it gone? Hey, answer! You!

Gerty An accident.

Blunderbore (*thumping the table*)
               You did this too!
               (*Shouting*) Fetch me some bread! Don't stand agog!
               (*He points at Gerty*)
               I'll eat *her* now, like a live hot dog!

Ferdy *Dog*, sir? Did you say hot dog? But she's a lady! Surely not *dog*.
Shouldn't that be hot—? Oh. No, perhaps not.

Two Guards enter bearing two enormous slices of bread

They put one piece of bread on the table and on this they place Gerty. On top of Gerty they place the other slice of bread—like a sandwich

Blunderbore That's far too big. Only one thing to do:
               Fetch me the knife and cut it in two.

The Guards get the knife and prepare to cut Gerty in half

Puss enters

Puss   Hold it, Ogre! Not so quick!
                     You eat all that and you'll be sick!
                     You'll get a nasty ulcer too.
                     Take care!
Blunderbore   And who the heck are you?
Puss   A magic cat! Of noble birth.
                     The cleverest Sorcerer on Earth.
Blunderbore   *A sorcerer?* Excuse my mirth.
                     You're not the cleverest on the Earth!
Puss   I am!
Blunderbore   You're not!
Puss   Then who is?
Blunderbore   Me!
Puss   Let's have a contest. Then we'll see!
Blunderbore   And if I win, I'll eat you too.
Puss   And if you don't, then I'll eat you!
Blunderbore   Eat me? Ha! That'll be the day.
                     Get this sandwich out of the way!

The Guards stand Gerty back with the others

                     Soon for mercy you'll be cryin'.
                     I'll change myself into a lion!

*Blunderbore raises his arms towards the ceiling. There is a roll of drums and the
Lights begin to fade as he chants*

                     Abra—cadabra! Abra—cadee!
                     Help yourself at the cafeteree!
                     Lyon's ices—Lyon's tea!
                     King of the Jungle I shall be!
                     Ha! Ha! Ha! Ha!

*There is a tremendous flash in front of Blunderbore, followed by a savage clap of
thunder and a Black-out. The drums and thunder continue. Blunderbore's
laughter continues but gradually dissolves into the roar of a lion*

*During the Black-out the actor playing the top half of Blunderbore slips
under the table. The Lion enters from behind the book and sits in
Blunderbore's chair. The Lion's voice is heard on the onstage speakers*

*The Lights snap on again. The Lion leaps from the chair and all present leap
back in fright as he growls at them all. The Lion chases Puss round the table and
finally Puss escapes by climbing up the wall—i.e. the rungs attached to the solid
flat. The Lion stands below Puss, snarling up at him*

Puss   Well, for an amateur, not bad.
                     It might have entertained me dad,
                     But frankly drives me up the wall!
                     Now change yourself to something small.

Lion Arrrrrrrrr?
Puss   It's always *monsters* with you chaps.
                Try something small—a mouse perhaps!

The Lion flaps his paw effeminately, as to say: "Easy!", and returns to his seat behind the table. Puss descends the wall. The Lion raises his paws and growls and roars. There is a roll of drums and the Lights fade. There is a flash, followed by thunder and then a Black-out. The Lion's roar dissolves into a high-pitched squeak

   During the Black-out the Lion exits

The Lights come up again. Everyone looks about for the mouse. Suddenly it appears from beneath the table, heading for the wings

Jack (*pointing*) There he is, look!

Puss leaps on to the mouse and swallows him. He rubs his tummy in triumph. The others are jubilant

                He's eaten him! He's eaten the Ogre!
Gerty What on earth do they taste like, Puss?
Puss (*with a twinge of indigestion*)
                Revolting! Specially when they're raw!
                Well, that's the end of Blunderbore!

The others begin to cheer, but the alarm bell sounds and Puss finds himself surrounded by the four Guards, their swords drawn. He draws his sword and engages all four. During the following fight everyone moves downstage and as soon as they are all clear the tabs close behind them, cutting off the rear half of the stage to facilitate the scene change

                Oh! These four would like to try their skill.
                Well, come in, Master, for the kill!

   Colin enters and engages two of the Guards fighting Puss

Isabel The Marquis!

Jack grabs the giant fork, and sticks it into the bottom of one of the Guards fighting Puss. He yells with pain, swings round, and engages with Jack

Gerty (*seeing this*) Good idea!

Gerty grabs the giant knife, and sticks it into the bottom of one of the Guards fighting Colin. He yells with pain, swings round, and engages with Gerty, who swings at his head with the most hair-raising swipes. Ferdy approaches the Guard fighting Gerty, and taps him on the shoulder

Guard (*turning*) Yes?
Ferdy Sir! *This* Is Your Life—I mean, my wife—I mean . . .

Gerty sticks the knife into the Guard's bottom again. He yells with pain, turns, and angrily re-engages with her. Ferdy kneels down behind the Guard. Gerty pushes the Guard in the chest with her knife, and he falls over Ferdy's back to c. *Jack's Guard backs and falls over Gerty's Guard. Puss's Guard backs and falls over Jack's Guard, and Colin's Guard backs and falls over all the Guards. The four Guards are now a helpless heap c, surrounded by Puss, Colin, Ferdy, Gerty and Jack. They seize the Guards' swords, lost in the general collapse*

Puss   Victory, Marquis! What success!
                 Now you must free the young Princess!
Colin (*removing Isabel's chains*) Allow me, Your Highness.
Puss (*to Guards*) Down in the dungeons you shall rot!
                 On your feet now! That's your lot!

The Guards rise and exit, followed by Puss and Jack

Isabel Thank you, Marquis. You fought bravely.
Gerty Well said, daughter. Ferdy, he ought to have a reward. (*To Colin*) What would you like, dear! (*She hands her knife to Ferdy*) Here come on, do your stuff. (*To Colin*) Kneel down, dear. (*To Ferdy*) Well, go on, knight him!
Ferdy Eh?
Gerty Make him Baron!
Ferdy (*startled*) I beg your pardon!
Gerty (*snatching the knife back*) Oh, here! (*She taps Colin on the shoulder with the knife*) Arise, Sir—— What's your name, dearie?
Colin Colin.
Gerty Arise, Sir Colin. Knight of the er—— what's it?
Ferdy Suspender!
Gerty Suspender—Garter! Now claim your reward.
Colin (*hesitating*) Your Majesty has already been too kind.
Gerty Come on! What do you want for a reward—as if we didn't know!
Colin Well then, Your Majesty—if she will accept me—may I claim your daughter's hand in marriage?

The music of Song 8 begins softly

Isabel (*delighted*) Sir Colin!
Gerty (*to Colin*) We thought you'd never say it! You'd better have the Ogre's castle and all, for a wedding present. Come on, Ferdy, let's find Jack.
Ferdy What, dear?

Gerty indicates that Colin and Isabel ought to be alone at a moment like this

          (*Misunderstanding*) Oh—arise, Sir Colin.
Gerty (*grabbing Ferdy by the collar*) Come on!

Gerty marches Ferdy off. They take the giant knife and fork with them

Isabel Colin.
Colin Princess.
Isabel (*mockingly*) Knight!
Colin Isabel!
Isabel Love.

Colin sings a reprise of Song 8

     At the end of the song they exit, arm in arm

     Puss enters from the opposite side and draws back the tabs to reveal:

SCENE 3

A gypsy encampment in the forest

Puss exits

The book is open depicting a gypsy encampment in the forest. There is lively gypsy music playing. Rosalind and Jill are seated on a log watching the gypsy dancers executing an exciting gypsy dance by the red glowing firelight. They pull Rosalind to her feet. At first she refuses but finally agrees to sing

Song 13

At the end of the dance the Gypsies exit

Jill That was wonderful, Your Highness.

Rosalind Your music is beautiful, Jill, but it cannot make me forget. We should have heard something by now.

Jill I am sure there is nothing to fear. I have spoken to Katranah—our Queen. She says the omens are good.

Rosalind She is a very old lady, isn't she?

Jill No-one knows how old she is. Some say more than a hundred and twenty years.

Rosalind She must be very wise.

Jill She is. She can see into the future as if it were the clearest stream. But see, they are bringing her here!

The Gypsies bring on the aged Katranah. She is ancient, croaking and wizened like a chewed lozenge and her head shakes continuously like an insecure blancmange. (This part could be played by an actor or actress) They seat her on the log, and the Gypsies exit

Katranah, Queen. I have been telling the Princess of your prophecies.

Katranah What prophecies, child?

Jill The return of our loved ones.

Rosalind Their fate at the castle.

Jack enters unseen by Jill

Katranah Why do you speak of prophecies. The River of Life must always flow into the Sea of the Future. See behind you!

Jill (*turning and seeing Jack*) Jack! Jack! You're alive!

She rushes into his arms

Jack Rather!

Rosalind But where are the others?

Gerty enters, followed by Ferdy, Colin and Isabel

Gerty We're here! And I'm watching you, Jack boy! Up to your tricks with the gypsies again!

Rosalind Mother!

Gerty Look at him! Around the girls in eighty ways!

Rosalind Mother, Father, are you all right?

Ferdy Oh, yes, daughter. Thanks to Sir Colin and his excellent cat. They dealt once and for all with that Ogue of a roguer—er, rogue of an Ogre!

Rosalind And you, sister, are you unharmed?

Isabel Except for my heart. I have lost that to my gallant rescuer. But I think it is safe, for we are to be married!

Rosalind Dearest sister, I am so happy!

Jack And that's what I'm going to do too!

Rosalind What, Jack?

Jack Marry the girl I love!

Gerty Oh no you're not. I shan't allow it. So there!

Jack Oh really, Mater. It's nothing to do with you!

Gerty Nothing to . . .! Well there's gratitude! If it weren't for taking off me velvet glove and showing me diamond ring to the atmosphere, I'd slap your saucy face!

Jack You can't stop us. This lady can marry us. You have no power over her!

Gerty Oh? Who's she?

Jack Queen of the Gypsies!

Gerty I thought it was one of the Brides of Dracula! (*All sweetness*) How d'you do. Lovely to meet you. (*To the others*) Is she nodding her head or imitating Elvis Presley? (*To Katranah*) If you're a gypsy, I wonder if you'd tell me my fortune.

Katranah holds out her hand. Gerty gives her hers

Oh goody! Excuse me filthy hands, I've been washing me face.

Katranah Cross me palm with silver.

Gerty Well, do you know I'm afraid I haven't actually got any silver at the moment. But I've got the top of a packet of corn flakes. If you send that up with fifty pence you . . .

Katranah Never mind. (*She peers into Gerty's hand*) Ah. You will be poor and unhappy until you are sixty!

Gerty Oh. What then?

Katranah You'll get used to it.

Gerty Well, I'm sure we all feel better for that!

Katranah (*taking out a pipe and matches*) Do you mind if I smoke?

Gerty I don't mind if you burst into flames!

Katranah Sharp, isn't she?

Ferdy When she was younger, ma'am, she was as sharp as a needle—except of course she was always being found in a haystack.

Katranah lights her pipe

Jack Well, Mater, which is it to be? Do you consent or not?

Gerty Well I don't know. She looks a nice healthy girl I must say.

Colin She is a princess, Your Majesty, after all.

Jack I shall never love anybody except Jill. If I wait any longer, nobody will love me. It'll be too late.

Gerty Oh, that's nonsense, dear!

Jack No, it isn't.
Gerty (*to Ferdy*) Shall we tell him?
Ferdy Just as you say, dearest.

Gerty and Ferdy sing

Song 14

Jack, Jill, Colin, Isabel and Rosalind all join in the number

Gerty All right! You win. You can marry your gypsy princess!

The others are all jubilant

That is if it's all right with Grandma Moses.

Katranah nods, and blows out a jet of smoke. Gerty gets a whiff of it and chokes

Ferdy, remind me to make this a smokeless zone. (*To Jack*) Though what you're going to live on, I don't know. I suppose you'll be selling pegs round the houses.
Jack Don't worry. We've got something put by for a rainy day!
Gerty Oh? What's that?

Jack produces an umbrella, which he opens. He and Jill stand under it

Well that's all right then. Phew! I'm dying of thirst. Here, let's have a swig of that milk. Then we can all go home. (*She approaches the milk*)
Audience Miaow!

Puss enters

Puss   Thanks, kids! I thought you might forget.
                    Your troubles, folks, aren't over yet.
                    I'm afraid you can't go home.
                    Gil and Filbert pinched your throne!
All What?
Puss   Convinced we'd seen our final hour,
                    When once within the Ogre's power,
                    Acting with their usual malice,
                    They've annexed the royal palace!
Isabel Oh no!
Puss   They gorge and drink and sleep all day,
                    And for this greed your subjects pay.
                    It's prison, or a heavy tax.
                    They steal the clothes from off their backs!
Colin Puss! What can we do? The palace will be guarded.
Puss   Thinking us dead, they're not afraid
                    That anyone would dare invade.
                    But we'll surprise them. Quickly too.
Colin   You're right. Come Jack, we've work to do!
Jill (*kissing Jack*) Take care.
Isabel (*kissing Colin*) Take care.

Ferdy holds out his lips to be kissed

Gerty Don't you kid yourself. You're staying here. Come on. (*She leads Ferdy off*) You know, you should have been a gypsy. You've always got that healthy browned-off look!

Ferdy and Gerty exit followed by Jill, Isabel and Rosalind who help Katranah off

Colin	Puss, I hope you've got a plan.
Jack	We're right behind you, to a man.
Colin	By horse we'll be there break of day. (*He starts to go*)
Puss	No, no! I know a quicker way.

Puss turns the page of the book to reveal:

SCENE 4

The throne room in the royal palace

Puss, Colin and Jack exit

Courtly music plays. Attendants enter with thrones which they place C. They exit and then re-enter with a table covered with chocolates, empty bottles of pop with straws, grapes, etc., etc., which they place in front of the thrones. They stand either side of the thrones

Gilbert and Filbert enter, sucking an ice-cream in one hand and a bottle of pop in the other. They are both wearing crowns and Gilbert has a whip. They sit on the thrones

Gilbert Who left that old log in here? Take it out! Find out who it was and execute him.

The Attendant exits with the log

(*To the other Attendant*) Here you! Peel me a grape.

The Attendant does so

Filbert, give us a chocolate.

Filbert sits with one leg cocked over the side of his throne. He passes some chocolates to Gilbert

The first Attendant enters

Attendant The peasants are here, Your Majesty, to pay their taxes. I'm afraid the executioner is nowhere to be found.
Filbert I wonder where he's got to?
Gilbert Perhaps he's gone for a walk round the block!

Gilbert and Filbert shriek with laughter

(*To the Attendant*) Here! Don't you think that's funny?
Attendant Yes, Your Majesty.

Gilbert Then laugh.

Attendant Ha! Ha! Ha! Your Majesty.

Gilbert That's better. Now then, call in the peasants. Let's see what they've got for us today.

Attendant (*calling off*) This way!

Three Peasants enter and stand before the thrones. The first has a turnip, the second has two marrows and the third has a basket of pomegranates

Gilbert (*cracking his whip*) On your knees! On your knees! Tut! You've got to tell 'em everything. What have you got?

1st Peasant My last turnip, Your Majesty.

Gilbert *One* turnip! *One* turnip! What do you think this is, harvest festival?

1st Peasant It's all I have, Your Majesty. Now I have nothing to eat at all.

Gilbert Chuck him in the dungeons. He can grow us some mushrooms.

The Attendant throws the Peasant out

The Peasant exits

(*Handing the turnip to Filbert*) Here you are. Here's a turnip for the book! (*He roars with laughter*) Oh, the devil's in me today. (*Angrily*) Laugh, peasants! (*He cracks his whip*)

Peasants
Attendants } (*together, miserably*) Ha! Ha! Ha!

Gilbert Louder! Ha! Ha! Ha!

Peasants
Attendants } (*together*) Ha! Ha! Ha!

Gilbert Next? What have you got?

2nd Peasant (*holding up two marrows*) Two marrow, Your Majesty.

Gilbert No, not tomorrow, today! Ha! Ha! Ha! (*To Peasants*) Ah? (*He cracks his whip*)

Peasants
Attendants } (*together, miserably*) Ha! Ha! Ha!

Gilbert (*pointing to one; accusingly*) You missed out a "Ha!". All right, we accept them. On condition you go out into the forest and fetch us a ham.

2nd Peasant A ham? But, Your Majesty, ham doesn't grow on trees.

Gilbert Oh, no? Never heard of an 'ambush? Quick! (*He cracks his whip*)

Peasants
Attendants } (*together*) Ha! Ha! Ha!

Gilbert That's better. All right, you, buzz off!

2nd Peasant exits

Next?

3rd Peasant Ten pomegranates, Your Majesty.

Gilbert Pomegranates! Oh, super slobby dobs! I love pomegranates. All right, 'op it. You needn't pay any more taxes for a week.

3rd Peasant exits

Gilbert picks up the pomegranates

Filbert Here! Fair do's, fair do's.
Gilbert All right, guzzle guts, cop hold! One for you. (*He gives one to Filbert*)
One for me. (*He takes one for himself*) Two for you. (*He gives Filbert
another one*) One, two for me. (*He takes another two for himself*) Three, for
you. (*He gives Filbert another one* (One, two, three, for me. (*He takes three
for himself. This leaves one which he gives to Filbert*) Four for you. (*Taking
all of Filbert's four*) One, two, three, four, for me. (*He now has ten and
Filbert none. To the Attendant*) Who's next?
Attendant Next?

*Puss, Colin and Jack enter, wearing long white beards and spectacles. They
each have swords concealed on them*

Gilbert What's this? The Darby and Joan Club? What have *you* brought me,
post-war credits?
Colin No, Your Majesty. I am an Inspector of Income Tax.
Gilbert (*aghast*) Income tax!
Colin (*indicating Jack*) My colleague, Carruthers from Customs and Excise.
Gilbert Customs and Excise!
Colin (*indicating Puss*) And Inspector Edie Puss, CID.
Filbert Whatcher, Sid!
Gilbert Quiet!
Colin You've been spending a lot of money!
Gilbert Well you know how it is. The price of things these days. Well I mean,
one small lettuce and half a bottle of gin, and bang goes a fiver!
Colin We have details of your income—most of it stolen, we understand—
and now we've brought you your return.
Gilbert ⎫ (*together*) What is our return?
Filbert ⎭
Colin (*drawing his sword*) This!

Puss and Jack draw their swords, and all three remove their disguises

Gilbert Ah, help!
Jack We can manage, we don't need any help.
Gilbert Guards! Guard us!

Gerty and Ferdy enter

Gerty That's right, guards, guard them. Take them down to the dungeons.
You can guard them better there.
Attendants (*delighted*) Certainly, Your Majesty!
Gilbert We thought you were dead!
Ferdy Ah! Counting your stitches before they've leaped!
Gerty Half a tick. I'll have me crown back first.

Colin and Puss remove the crowns from Gilbert and Filbert

Gilbert You wait! I'll pay you for this!
Jack Quite right, you will. Probably with your heads!

The Attendants march Gilbert and Filbert off

Colin Your Majesties, your thrones are safe!

There is a long, splendid fanfare of trumpets. Ferdy and Gerty ascend their thrones. Colin and Puss place the crowns on the royal couple's heads

> *Isabel, Rosalind, Jill, Ladies and Gentlemen of the Court, Peasants, Attendants, etc., etc., enter and kneel before the thrones. When the fanfare stops they sing a reprise of Song 2*

All (*singing*)   Hail to His Majesty,
King Ferdinand of Hearts.
Hail to Queen Gertrude,
Who made the Royal tarts.
Hail to the head,
That wears the Royal Crown,
Hail to Ferd and Gerty
They never let us down!

The Court rises to its feet

Ferdy (*rising*) Er, Ladles and Jellyspoons—I er, come before you, to—er—stand behind you—to tell you something . . . I know nothing about . . . (*He catches Gerty's eye*) Yes, dear! (*He sits*)

Gerty (*rising*) People of this realm, once more we acclaim the champion of our land, Sir Colin, Marquis of Carabas, henceforth Prince Colin of our Court!

Everyone cheers

Colin Thanks to Your Majesty, but the credit is not mine. Your Majesty's true champion is Puss in Boots!

Jack Yes, Mater. What is *his* reward to be?

Gerty Well, Puss, what *is* it to be? Name it and it shall be granted.

Puss hesitates

Jack Come, Puss, anything you wish!

Puss   Your Majesty will grant me all?
Anything? Without recall?

Gerty   You have but to command.

Puss   Four wishes Queen.

Gerty   All you desire.

Puss   My milk! That burns with magic fire.

Gerty   Of course, what else?

Puss   My master's sword!

Colin (*giving Puss his sword*)
          An honour Puss, but small reward.

Puss   Princess Rosalind for wife!

There is a gasp from the Court and Puss kneels before Rosalind

         Who with this sword must take my life!

There is general dismay. The melody of Song 9 begins

Colin   Puss! What are you saying?
Jack   This cannot be!
Gerty (*distressed*) What can I do?
Puss (*staring into Rosalind's eyes*) Remember me!

Rosalind, almost hypnotized, sings the refrain from Song 9

Isabel   What is it, sister?
Rosalind   I agree!
Gerty (*wretchedly*) I can't refuse. This thing must be!

*There is a roll of drums. Puss takes up the milk and drinks. He kneels before
Rosalind again. She slowly raises the sword, then strikes Puss. There is a flash
of smoke! Black-out! When the Lights snap on again, where Puss was kneeling,
a handsome Marquis stands before Rosalind. There is general astonishment*

Rosalind You! I knew . . . the eyes . . .
Gerty Well I'll go to our house.
Jack But, Puss . . .
Colin *Who are you?*
Marquis The Marquis of Carabas!
Gerty What another one?
Marquis The real one I assure you. My lands were stolen by the Ogre. I was
    captured, and with his magic power he turned me into a cat! But I learned
    the only way to break his spell was to be struck with a mortal blow from the
    one I loved.
Rosalind You were fleeing from the Ogre's men when I saw you in the forest.
Marquis   It was but a moment before I was captured.
                     The worst thing of the Ogre's curse
                     Was speaking in that ghastly verse!
Jack Aha! He's at it again.

They all laugh

Gerty And so you love our Rosalind?
Marquis With Your Majesty's leave.
Gerty Splendid! Splendid!
Rosalind No, Mother, not splendid—splendoured!
Gerty What do you mean, dear?
Rosalind (*smiling to Colin*) Your Highness?
Colin (*bowing*) Your Highness!

They sing—Colin to Isabel, Rosalind to the Marquis—a reprise of Song 7

Gerty Ferdy!
Ferdy Yes, dear?
Gerty We've got to celebrate. We'll have a ball.
Ferdy When, dear?
Gerty Right now!

Everyone cheers

    I love balls, Marquis. Did you know I met my husband at a ball? It was a
    terrible shock.

Marquis Why, Your Majesty?
Gerty I thought he was at home minding the kids. Music!

Song 1 (Reprise)

The orchestra play a reprise of Song 1 and they all sing and dance

  During this the thrones and tables are cleared

On the final lines of the song, the Marquis walks up to the book and the whole Company turn to face him. He turns the last page. It reads: THE END

CURTAIN

SCENE 5

Walkdown and Finale

As the Finale music starts the Company walk down, take their bows and then sing

Final Chorus

CURTAIN

FURNITURE AND PROPERTY LIST

On stage: Giant book (closed)

Off stage: Noticeboard attached to artificial ice-crack, fishing-rod and line attached to artificial hole **(Puss)**

ACT I

SCENE 1

On stage: Giant book

Off stage: Bucket **(Jill)**
Bucket containing solid block of ice **(Jack)**
School bell **(Mr Tap)**
Toboggan **(Colin)**
Schoolbooks **(Gilbert** and **Filbert)**

Personal: **Jack:** crown
Ferdy: spectacles, crown
Gerty: roller skates, crown

SCENE 2

On stage: Giant book

Off stage: Long benches, comic bench, blackboard with letters of alphabet on it and nail, easel, cane, etc. **(Children)**
School bell **(Mr Tap)**
Scrubbing brush on lead **(Filbert)**
Will **(Gilbert)**

Personal: **Jack:** eye patch, hat
Ferdy: spectacles, crown
Gerty: crown
Colin: coin in pocket

SCENE 3

On stage: Giant book

Off stage: Tray of boots including **Puss**'s red thigh-length boots **(Cobbler)**
Saucer of milk **(Puss)**
Sack **(Puss)**

SCENE 4

On stage: Giant book
           Saucer of milk
           Tree cut-out

Off stage: Large sack with string attached to neck, cuckoo clock **(Puss)**
            Whip **(Gilbert)**
            Twig **(Filbert)**

Personal: **Gilbert:** sword
           Filbert: sword, box of powder, pencil

SCENE 5

Strike   Tree cut-out

On stage: Giant book
           Saucer of milk

Off stage: Small spinet with loose key **(Isabel** and **Rosalind)**
            Stool, music **(Ferdy)**
            Large sack containing stuffed animals tied at the neck **(Puss)**
            Cello **(Gilbert)**
            Recorder **(Filbert)**

Personal: **Ferdy:** spectacles, straw in pocket, crown
           Filbert: music in pocket

SCENE 6

On stage: Giant book
           Saucer of milk

Off stage: Bundle of wood **(Jill)**
            Axe **(Woodcutter)**
            Dog on lead **(Puss)**
            Spears, various hunting weapons **(Attendants)**

Personal: **Ferdy:** sou'wester, spectacles, sword
           Colin: sword
           Puss: sword

ACT II

SCENE 1

On stage: Giant book (open)
           Saucer of milk
           Clock cut-out with large bell. *Behind clock:* 2 hammers, long white beard
             for **Jack**
           Mirrorframe
           Laundry basket. *In it:* 3 "ghost" sheets with headpieces

Off stage: Swords **(Guards)**

Personal: **Ghost:** ball and chain
               Ghost: hat
               Ghost: false head
               Ferdy: spectacles
               Ghost: sundial on chain
               Colin: sword
               Puss: sword

SCENE 2

Strike: Mirrorframe
         Laundry basket

On stage: Giant book (open)
          Saucer of milk
          Giant table covered with tablecloth. *On it:* giant knife, fork, plate and
            hollow cup
          Large oven
          3 tall cages

Off stage: Large trolley. *On it:* 11 metal plates, 1 cardboard plate, large jar of yeast,
          bowl with lump of dough, strong paper bag containing flour, 2 full soda
          syphons **(Guards)**
          Mouse **(Stage management)**

Personal: **Guards:** swords
         Ferdy: spectacles
         Guard: large handkerchief
         Isable: chains
         Puss: sword
         Colin: sword

SCENE 3

On stage: Giant book (open)
          Saucer of milk
          Log

Personal: **Katranah:** pipe and tobacco, matches
         Jack: umbrella
         Ferdy: spectacles

SCENE 4

On stage: Giant book
          Saucer of milk

Off stage: 2 thrones **(Attendants)**
          Table. *On it:* chocolates, empty pop bottles with straws, grapes, etc.
          (Attendants)
          Ice cream, bottle of pop, whip **(Gilbert)**
          Ice cream, bottle of pop **(Filbert)**
          Turnip **(1st Peasant)**
          2 marrows **(2nd Peasant)**
          Basket containing 10 pomegranates **(3rd Peasant)**

Personal: **Gilbert:** crown
             Filbert: crown
             Puss: long white beard, spectacles, sword
             Colin: long white beard, spectacles, sword
             Jack: long white beard, spectacles, sword
             Ferdy: spectacles

SCENE 5

On stage: Giant book

LIGHTING PLOT

The following plot indicates those lighting changes and effects specified in the text. These may be elaborated at the discretion of the director

Property fittings required: nil
Various simple interior and exterior settings

PROLOGUE

To open: General bright daylight effect

No cues

ACT I

To open: General bright daylight effect

Cue 1	**Gerty:** ". . . it gives me great pleasure . . ." *Darken lighting*	(Page 6)
Cue 2	**Puss** turns the page of the book *Bring up general interior lighting*	(Page 7)
Cue 3	**Puss** turns the page of the book *Change to general exterior lighting*	(Page 14)
Cue 4	**Puss** turns the page of the book *Change to forest lighting*	(Page 18)
Cue 5	**Gilbert** hops about holding his foot *Darken lighting*	(Page 21)
Cue 6	**Filbert** covers his eyes and shakes *Change to forest lighting as before*	(Page 22)
Cue 7	**Puss** turns the page of the book *Change to interior lighting*	(Page 23)
Cue 8	**Puss** turns back the page of the book *Change to forest lighting*	(Page 30)

ACT II

To open: Gloomy interior lighting

Cue 9	**Puss** appears to pull back the tabs *Change to dim interior lighting*	(Page 42)
Cue 10	**Blunderbore** raises his arms towards the ceiling *Start fade*	(Page 49)
Cue 11	Flash and savage clap of thunder *Black-out*	(Page 49)

EFFECTS PLOT

ACT I

Cue 1	As **Children** play leapfrog *Sound of bucket crashing*	(Page 3)
Cue 2	**Mr Tap:** "... to speak to those boys." *Motor horn*	(Page 4)
Cue 3	**Gilbert:** "Did you say the Queen?" *Trumpet fanfare*	(Page 5)
Cue 4	**Gerty:** "... cheeldrenn (*a crocodile smile*) ..." *Thunder rumbles*	(Page 6)
Cue 5	**Gerty:** "... it gives me great pleasure ..." *Louder thunder*	(Page 6)
Cue 6	**Children** and **Villagers** rush off behind the mill *Thunder*	(Page 7)
Cue 7	**Blunderbore** growls *Thunder*	(Page 7)
Cue 8	**Puss** pulls on his boots *Hiss of cymbals*	(Page 15)
Cue 9	**Puss** sets the clock going *Loud "tick-tock" noise. Continue until* **Puss** *exits*	(Page 19)
Cue 10	**Gilbert:** (off): "Go on, Oswald. Giddyap!" *Whip crack*	(Page 19)
Cue 11	**Blunderbore** (*off*): "... feeble bones to dust." *Loud thunderclap*	(Page 22)
Cue 12	Fading cries of **Gilbert** and **Filbert** off *Loud splash*	(Page 30)
Cue 13	**Filbert:** "Ha! Ha! Ha! *Trumpet sounds far off*	(Page 32)
Cue 14	**Puss** and the dog exit *Trumpet fanfare*	(Page 33)
Cue 15	**Filbert** rushes off after **Gilbert** *Horses galloping away*	(Page 36)

ACT II

Cue 16	To open SCENE 1 *Ghostly effects. Cut as music changes*	(Page 38)

| *Cue* 17 | As **Gerty**, **Ferdy** and **Jack** reach c | (Page 38) |
| | *Loud clockwork rattling effect* | |

| *Cue* 18 | As **Father Time** and **Cupid** strike bell | (Page 38) |
| | *Half-hour bell* | |

| *Cue* 19 | As **Ferdy** and **Jack** strike bell | (Page 39) |
| | *Bell sounds* | |

| *Cue* 20 | **Gerty:** "I don't want any of that!" | (Page 41) |
| | *Loud alarm bell* | |

| *Cue* 21 | **Blunderbore** (*off*) "... my castle lair?" | (Page 41) |
| | *Loud gong* | |

| *Cue* 22 | **Jack** switches on the oven | (Page 47) |
| | *Hissing noise followed by the opening of Strauss's "Thus Spake Zarathustra"** | |

| *Cue* 23 | **Blunderbore** raises his arms to the ceiling | (Page 49) |
| | *Drum roll* | |

| *Cue* 24 | **Blunderbore:** "Ha! Ha! Ha! Ha!" | (Page 49) |
| | *Flash, then thunderclap. Then drums and thunder continue until Lights come up again* | |

| *Cue* 25 | **Lion** roars and growls | (Page 50) |
| | *Drum roll, followed by flash, then thunder* | |

| *Cue* 26 | The others begin to cheer | (Page 50) |
| | *Loud alarm bell* | |

| *Cue* 27 | **Colin:** "... your thrones are safe!" | (Page 58) |
| | *Loud trumpet fanfare* | |

| *Cue* 28 | **Gerty:** "... this thing must be!" | (Page 59) |
| | *Drum roll* | |

| *Cue* 29 | **Rosalind** strikes **Puss** | (Page 59) |
| | *Flash box* | |

*A licence issued by Samuel French Ltd to perform this play does not include permission to use copyright recorded material. A separate and additional licence from Phonographic Performances Ltd, Granton House, Granton Street, London W1, is needed whenever commercial recordings are used.

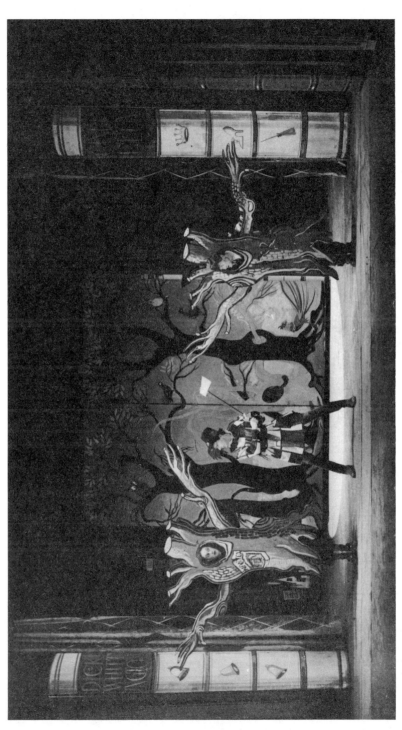

ACT I. SCENE 6

Photograph by Brian Douglas

ACT II. SCENE 2

Photograph by Brian Douglas

MADE AND PRINTED IN GREAT BRITAIN BY
LATIMER TREND & COMPANY LTD PLYMOUTH
MADE IN ENGLAND